A Handbook of Structured Experiences for Human Relations Training

Volume IX

Edited by

J. WILLIAM PFEIFFER, Ph.D.

UNIVERSITY ASSOCIATES
Publishers and Consultants
8517 Production Avenue
San Diego, California 92121

SERIES IN HUMAN RESOURCE DEVELOPMENT

Copyright © 1983 by International Authors, B.V.

ISBN: 0-88390-049-1

Library of Congress Catalog Card Number 73-92840

The materials that appear in this book (except those for which reprint permission must be obtained from the primary sources) may be reproduced for educational/training activities. Special permission for such uses is not required. However, we do ask that the following statement appear on all reproductions:

This permission statement is limited to the reproduction of materials for educational/training events. *Systematic* or *large-scale reproduction* or distribution—or inclusion of items in publications for sale—may be done only with prior written permission.

Printed in the United States of America

PREFACE

In the fourteen years since the publication of Volume I of this series, a vast quantity of related material has passed across my desk. It seems to me that more structured experiences are being developed now than at any time before.

I remain concerned that this new volume not be dominated by variations of previously published structured experiences. There are, however, a few variations, which will allow you to continue to use favorites but add new content that is of a more current theme and to avoid the mechanical repetition that sometimes accompanies the overuse of any learning experience. For the most part, the structured experiences in this volume are fresh ways to help us to focus awareness and enhance our understanding of the world in which we live. I remain enthusiastic about the potential for learning from this type of experience and the accompanying publishing, processing, generalizing, and applying.

This volume, like its predecessors, contains twenty-four structured experiences. Users are encouraged to adapt and modify them to suit their own unique needs and circumstances. In producing this volume, we have tried to make the designs as generally applicable as possible, trying to avoid those suited only to relatively specialized uses.

We at University Associates continue to hold the professional value that resources should be shared by peers. The *Handbooks of Structured Experiences for Human Relations Training* are one important evidence of this belief. We continue to invite users to participate in this process, through feedback suggestions and by sending us materials that have proven helpful to them. As with all University Associates publications, users may freely reproduce these materials for educational or training purposes. For large-scale distribution or the inclusion of materials in publications for sale, prior written permission is required.

I am very appreciative of the editorial system that has made this volume of the *Handbook* possible. I particularly wish to thank Len Goodstein for his counsel in selecting the activities, Beverly Byrum-Gaw for her user-oriented content consultation, and finally Carol Nolde for the patience and dedication that made a stack of papers a book.

J. William Pfeiffer

San Diego, California
March, 1983

TABLE OF CONTENTS

---

*See Introduction, p. 3, for explanation of numbering.

INTRODUCTION

Our early work in creating learning designs led us to the use of what had always been termed "exercises," "techniques," or "games." When we made the decision to gather these valuable materials into a book, we became concerned that "exercise" and "game" had connotations we considered dysfunctional to the intent of their use. We therefore elected to call them "structured experiences," to indicate that they are designed for experience-based learning.

Our interest in providing participants with a distinctive design for human relations training has resulted in an increasing orientation in our consulting activities, laboratories, and workshops toward experiences that produce generally predictable outcomes. In designing human relations training experiences, we strive to become aware of and to examine the specific needs of the client system or particular group and then develop learning situations that will meet those needs. Based on an experiential model, structured experiences are inductive rather than deductive, providing *direct* rather than vicarious learnings. Thus, participants *discover* meaning for themselves and *validate* their own experience.

A variety of experiential learning models have been developed in recent years (see Palmer, 1981). Our own version has five steps that occur in a cycle:

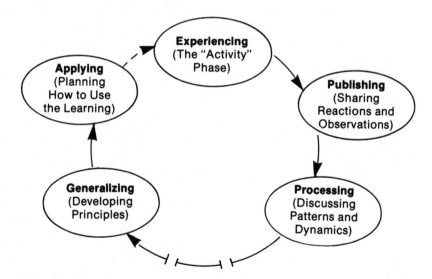

The *experiencing* phase involves some activity such as fantasy, dyadic sharing, or group problem solving. If the model stopped at this point, however, training would be only "fun and games." Next the participants engage in *publishing* their reactions to and observations of the activity. This is the data-generation phase; it leads logically into *processing*. It is our belief that processing is the key to the potency of structured experiences, and it is important that the facilitator allow sufficient time for this step. If the training is to transfer to the "real world," it is important for the participants to be able to extrapolate the experience from a laboratory setting to the outside world through *generalizing*. In this phase participants develop principles, hypotheses, and generalizations that can be discussed in the final phase, *applying*. This final phase must not be left to chance; facilitators need to ensure that participants recognize the relevance of the learning. The actual application of behavior becomes a new experience and begins the cycle again.

There is no successful way to cut short this cycle. If structured experiences are to be effective, the facilitator must supply adequate opportunities for "talk-through." The payoff comes when the participants learn *useful* things that they take responsibility for applying.

Thus, a concern that we bring to all our training publications is the need for adequate processing of the training experience so that participants are able to integrate the learning without the stress generated by unresolved feelings about the experience. It is at this point that the expertise of the facilitator becomes crucial if the experience is to be responsive to the learning and emotional needs of the participants. The facilitator must judge whether he or she will be able successfully to process the data that probably will emerge in the group through the structured experience. Any facilitator, regardless of background, who is committed to the growth of individuals in the group can usefully employ structured experiences. The choice of a particular activity must be made using two criteria: the facilitator's competence and the participants' needs.

As in the previous volumes of the *Handbook,* the sequencing of structured experiences in Volume IX has been based on the amount of understanding, skill and experience needed by the facilitator to use each experience effectively. The first structured experience, therefore, requires much less background on the part of the facilitator than does the last. The earlier experiences generate less affect and less data than do those near the end of the book, and, consequently, the facilitator needs less skill in processing to use them effectively and responsibly.

It is also the responsibility of the facilitator to examine the specific needs and the level of sophistication of the group and to choose a suitable structured experience. Adaptability and flexibility are, therefore, emphasized in the design of the structured experiences in this volume. The variations listed after each structured experience suggest possible alterations that a facilitator may wish to incorporate in order to make the experience more suitable to the particular design and to the needs of the participants. The expected norm in human relations training is innovation.

Our use of and experimentation with structured experiences led us to an interest in developing useful, uncomplicated questionnaires, opinionnaires, and other instruments. It is our belief that instruments enhance and reinforce the learning from structured experiences. Instruments also provide feedback to the facilitator on the appropriateness of the activity and the effectiveness of the presentation.

Some instruments appeared in the first volumes of these *Handbooks* and have subsequently been revised and refined in later editions. Each volume of the *Handbooks* contains structured experiences that include instruments. We find that the complementary selection of structured experiences and instruments can create powerful learning environments for participants, and we encourage those involved in the field of human relations training to become acquainted with this twofold approach in providing for participants' learning needs.

At the end of each structured experience in this volume are cross references to similar structured experiences, suggested instruments, and lecturette sources that seem especially appropriate to that experience. The number of each supplemental or complementary structured experience and the publication in which it appears are indicated. Instruments and lecturettes are listed by title and publication. Space for notes on each structured experience has been provided for the convenience of the facilitator.

Our published structured experiences are numbered consecutively throughout the series of *Handbooks* and *Annuals,* in order of publication of the volumes. A list of all structured experiences by category is found at the end of this book. This category system was developed for *The Structured Experience Kit,* which contains structured experiences from all volumes of the *Handbook* and all volumes of the *Annual.* One feature of the *Kit* is that each experience has been rated according to (a) how much affect is likely to be generated, (b) how structurally complex the design is, and (c) how difficult the activity is to process.

The contents of the entire series of *Handbooks* and *Annuals* are fully indexed in the revised *Reference Guide to Handbooks and Annuals.* The *Reference Guide* is an indispensable aid in locating a particular structured experience or a structured experience for a particular purpose, as well as related instruments, lecturettes, and theory articles.

The purpose, then, of the *Handbooks* is to share further the training materials that we have found to be useful in training designs. Some of the experiences that appear here originated within University Associates, and some were submitted to us by facilitators in the field. It is gratifying to find that facilitators around the world are using the *Handbooks* and concur with our philosophy that sharing these valuable materials with others is far more in the spirit of human relations theory than the stagnating concept of "ownership" of ideas.

Users are encouraged to submit structured experiences, instruments they have developed, and papers they have written that might be of interest to practitioners in human relations training. In this manner, our Series in Human Relations Training will continue to serve as a clearinghouse for ideas developed by group facilitators.

REFERENCE

Palmer, A. Learning cycles: Models of behavioral change. In J. E. Jones & J. W. Pfeiffer (Eds.), *The 1981 annual handbook for group facilitators.* San Diego, CA: University Associates, 1981.

341. SYNONYMS:
SHARING PERCEPTIONS BETWEEN GROUPS

Goals

I. To offer two different groups an opportunity to compare the ways in which they perceive and talk about their worlds.

II. To illustrate that people's language both expands and limits their worlds.

III. To improve understanding between two groups.

Group Size

A group of management personnel and a group of nonmanagement personnel. Each group should consist of no more than twelve members.

Time Required

Approximately one hour.

Materials

I. A newsprint flip chart and a felt-tipped marker for each group.

II. Masking tape.

Physical Setting

A room large enough so that the two groups can work separately without being overheard by each other.

Process

I. The facilitator asks the participants to form two groups according to their job functions: management and nonmanagement.

II. Each group is given a newsprint flip chart and a felt-tipped marker and is asked to select a recorder. It is explained that each recorder is to maintain a newsprint list while the group generates as many synonyms as possible for the nouns *manager* and *subordinate*. (Fifteen minutes.)

III. The total group is reconvened, and the recorders are asked to post their lists side by side so that the synonyms can be viewed by all of the participants.

IV. The facilitator leads a concluding discussion by asking the following questions:

1. Which synonyms elicit positive feelings? Which elicit negative feelings?
2. Which synonyms seem to limit the original terms? Which expand the terms?
3. Which synonyms indicate similarities in perception between the two groups? Which indicate differences? How might these similarities and differences affect the relationship between management and nonmanagement personnel?
4. Which synonyms imply perceptions that you were not aware existed? How might your new awareness be used productively?
5. Did you or your group experience any difficulty in generating synonyms? If so, what was the nature of this difficulty? What does it indicate about your perceptions of the two groups?
6. What have you learned about your own functioning as a manager or a subordinate?
7. How can you apply what you have learned to your work environment?

Variations

I. Instead of using the words *manager* and *subordinate* as the basis for generating synonyms, the participants may be asked to work with any of the following terms:

compromise	authority
decision making	organization development
participatory management	leadership
feedback	team building
deadline	conflict
goals	top management
collaboration	performance appraisal
production	priorities
time management	meetings
co-workers	transfer

II. The activity may be continued after Step IV by having the participants form groups of mixed composition and asking them to generate synonyms for terms that imply working together, such as *collaboration, integration, cooperation,* and so forth. Then the task should be processed in terms of similarities and differences in both product and process.

III. The activity may be used with groups that represent other types of differences in composition, such as opposite sexes, different races, or different ethnic groups. In such a case, the terms used to generate synonyms should be changed accordingly.

Similar Structured Experiences: *Vol. III:* Structured Experience **68**; *Vol. VII:* **250**; *'81 Annual:* **289**.

Lecturette Sources: *73 Annual:* "Conditions Which Hinder Effective Communication"; *78 Annual:* "Communicating Communication."

Notes on the Use of "Synonyms":

Submitted by Phil Leamon.

342. NEWS BULLETIN: FOCUSING THE GROUP

Goals

I. To develop readiness for interaction at the beginning of a group session.

II. To free group members from personal concerns so that they can concentrate on group matters.

Group Size

All members of an ongoing group.

Time Required

Approximately five minutes per member: two or three minutes for sharing of personal concerns plus another two or three minutes for group discussion of these concerns. (This time may need to be expanded in order to accomplish Goal II.)

Physical Setting

Any room in which the group regularly meets.

Process

I. The facilitator introduces the activity by pointing out that occasionally television newscasters interrupt regularly scheduled programs to make announcements and then state that details will be provided later. It is explained that such interruptions are distracting in two ways: They detract from the viewers' enjoyment of the interrupted programs, and they pique curiosity about issues that are not clarified at the time. The facilitator then states that a similar situation sometimes occurs during sessions attended by ongoing groups; while important group business is being conducted, members interject distracting comments about personal concerns.

II. The facilitator proposes a solution to this dilemma by suggesting that the group members share their personal concerns and "news items" at the outset of each session, before group matters are dealt with. Then the participants are invited to take turns spending two or three minutes revealing whatever personal concerns they wish. After each participant's turn, interaction is encouraged. (The facilitator should monitor each interaction period carefully so that the group members neither stray from the subject at hand nor force attention away from the individual who has just finished sharing.)

III. The facilitator directs the participants' attention to group matters.

Variations

I. The participants may be given the option of simply sharing their feelings and concerns and explaining as much as they wish without receiving responses from the other group members.

II. The time requirement for the activity may be reduced by asking each participant to complete the phrase "Right now I am..." in one sentence.

III. The facilitator may specify that the participants share their feelings in short comments concerning a specific subject, such as issues that are presently causing confusion, irritation, or happiness.

IV. Between Steps II and III, the facilitator may lead a brief discussion by eliciting answers to questions such as the following:

1. What did the sharing of personal concerns accomplish for you? for the group?
2. What are the advantages and disadvantages of this sharing procedure?
3. How might the procedure help the group to improve its functioning?

Lecturette Sources: *74 Annual:* "Hidden Agendas"; *75 Annual:* "Wishes and Fears."

Notes on the Use of "News Bulletin":

Submitted by Fred E. Woodall.

343. BRICKS: CREATIVE PROBLEM SOLVING

Goals

I. To provide the participants with an opportunity to practice creative problem solving.

II. To allow the participants to experience the dynamics that are involved in group-task accomplishment.

Group Size

Three to five groups of four to seven participants each.

Time Required

Approximately one and one-half hours.

Materials

I. A copy of the Bricks Task Sheet for each participant.

II. A newsprint flip chart and a felt-tipped marker for each group.

III. Masking tape.

Physical Setting

A room large enough to allow the groups to complete their task without disturbing one another.

Process

I. The participants are assembled into three to five groups of four to seven each.

II. Each participant is given a copy of the Bricks Task Sheet and is asked to read the handout.

III. The facilitator elicits and answers questions about the task and reads the following guidelines for creative problem solving:[1]

1. Adopt a questioning attitude.

---

[1]Adapted from M.B. Ross, "Creativity and Creative Problem Solving," in J.E. Jones and J.W. Pfeiffer (Eds.), *The 1981 Annual Handbook for Group Facilitators,* University Associates, 1981.

2. Establish an environment of acceptance in which ideas are considered before they are judged.

3. Examine the problem from new angles; try stating it in atypical ways.

4. Break the problem into its components and list as many alternatives as possible for each component; combine the alternatives to create new variations.

Each group is provided with a newsprint flip chart and a felt-tipped marker so that ideas can be recorded as the members work. Then the groups are told that they have fifteen minutes to accomplish the task and are invited to begin.

IV. After fifteen minutes each group is instructed to stop its work and to prepare a five-minute presentation of its ideas for the total group. The facilitator suggests that newsprint posters be created as visual aids for the presentations. (Ten minutes.)

V. The groups take turns delivering their presentations. Masking tape is provided so that the groups can display their posters.

VI. The facilitator leads a discussion of the entire activity by eliciting answers to the following questions:

1. What method did your group use to generate ideas? What was helpful about this method? What was not helpful?

2. How was your group's approach "creative"?

3. Did everyone in your group participate equally? If not, why did some members participate more than others? What effect did the members' levels of participation have on the group's ability to solve the problem creatively?

4. How might this activity relate to problem solving at work? at home?

5. What might be a first step toward incorporating creative problem solving into your back-home situation?

Variations

I. Each group may be asked to generate uses for a specified quantity of a different material. Such materials may include packages of licorice whips, balls of yarn, can openers, and boxes of uncooked spaghetti.

II. The facilitator may specify that the groups use brainstorming to accomplish their task.

III. Issues related to competition among groups may be emphasized during the activity and the processing.

Similar Structured Experiences: *Vol. III:* Structured Experience **53**; *77 Annual:* **185**; *79 Annual:* **240**; *'81 Annual:* **285**; *'83 Annual:* **335**.

Suggested Instrument: *78 Annual:* "Phases of Integrated Problem Solving (PIPS)."

Lecturette Sources: *'80 Annual:* "A Nine-Step Problem-Solving Model"; *'81 Annual:* "Creativity and Creative Problem Solving"; *'83 Annual:* "A Guide to Problem Solving."

Notes on the Use of "Bricks":

Submitted by J. Allan Tyler.

BRICKS TASK SHEET

Your group has just been stranded without provisions on a deserted island. In your search for supplies, you and your fellow members locate a little food and two thousand bricks. In discussing the situation, the group determines that rescue probably will not occur for at least two weeks and that the food is insufficient to support everyone for that period. Therefore, the members decide that the task of immediate importance is to generate creative ways of using the bricks to increase chances for survival.

344. ALL IOWANS ARE NAIVE: BREAKING CULTURAL STEREOTYPES

Goals

I. To increase the participants' awareness of the stereotypes that they hold.

II. To provide the participants with an opportunity to share their feelings about being the objects of stereotyping.

III. To allow the participants to observe how others feel when they are negatively stereotyped.

Group Size

Five to ten dyads. (This activity is best used with a well-established, mature group.)

Time Required

Approximately one and one-half hours.

Materials

I. A copy of the All Iowans Are Naive City-and-State Combinations (enough combinations to accommodate all dyads). Prior to conducting the activity, the facilitator should cut these combinations along the horizontal and vertical dashed lines so that on each resulting slip of paper is the name of a city *or* a state. Then the facilitator should stack the slips of paper in such a way that no city is directly above or below its state.

II. Enough stereotypical statements to accommodate all dyads. The facilitator can elect to use statements from one of the four sheets—the All Iowans Are Naive Regional Stereotypes, the All Iowans Are Naive Occupational Stereotypes, the All Iowans Are Naive Ethnic-Group Stereotypes, or the All Iowans Are Naive Gender Stereotypes—or a combination of statements from more than one sheet. Before conducting the activity, the facilitator should cut the chosen statements along the horizontal and vertical dashed lines so that on each resulting slip of paper is the object of a stereotype (for example, "All Southerners") *or* a stereotypical image (for example, "are hillbillies"). After the statements have been cut apart, the slips of paper should be stacked in such a way that no object of a stereotype is directly above or below its stereotypical image.

III. Blank paper and a pencil for each participant.

Physical Setting

A room with plenty of space so that the participants can move around freely. A writing surface also should be provided for each participant.

Process

I. The facilitator distributes the slips of paper on which are printed the names of cities or states. Each participant is instructed to find the person in the room whose slip of paper pairs with his or hers to form an accurate city-and-state combination. (For example, the person whose slip of paper reads "Spokane" should locate the person whose slip of paper reads "Washington.")

II. When everyone has found a partner, the facilitator asks each dyad to tell the group its city-and-state match. The group, in turn, indicates whether the match is correct. (This phase of the activity serves as a warm-up and prepares the participants for the next step.)

III. The facilitator distributes the slips of paper on which are printed the objects of stereotypes or stereotypical images. Each participant is instructed to find the person in the room whose slip of paper pairs with his or hers to form a complete, stereotypical statement. The facilitator should emphasize that each participant must find a match and that both people must agree on any given match.

IV. When all participants have found partners, the facilitator asks each dyad to recheck its sentence silently to confirm the match. At this time the participants should be given a chance to make other matches if they are not content with their original choices.

V. The dyads take turns reading their sentences aloud. After each sentence is read, the participants are asked to respond by stating what they think of the sentence, how they feel about it, and whether they believe it is true. (Twenty minutes.)

VI. After all sentences have been read and responses have been made, the facilitator leads a discussion about stereotypes. The following questions should be included:

1. What are stereotypes?
2. How do we form stereotypes (either negative or positive)?
3. What purpose do stereotypes serve?
4. What effect do stereotypes have on those being stereotyped? on those espousing the stereotypes?
5. How can we break the stereotypes that we have formed?

(Twenty minutes.)

VII. When the discussion has been concluded, the facilitator distributes blank sheets of paper and pencils. The participants are instructed to write five negative ways in which they and/or groups they represent have been stereotyped (either during this activity or previously). (Ten minutes.)

VIII. The participants are then assembled into groups of four or five each and are asked to share their written stereotypes and to discuss how they feel about them and what they might be able to do about them. (Fifteen minutes.)

IX. The total group is reconvened, and the facilitator elicits the participants' ideas regarding productive action that can be taken to reduce stereotyping.

Variations

I. A different type of warm-up may be substituted for the activity involving the city-and-state combinations, or the facilitator may begin the structured experience with Step III.

II. The experience may be adapted for use in an office setting by dealing exclusively with stereotypes about administrators, office managers, secretaries, typists, filing clerks, and so forth.

III. With an ongoing or a newly formed work group, the facilitator may elect to use only stereotypes that might affect relationships within the group.

Similar Structured Experiences: *'73 Annual:* Structured Experience **95**; *'76 Annual:* **184**; *Vol. VI:* **213**; *Vol. VII:* **247, 258, 262**; *'80 Annual:* **273**; *'81 Annual:* **292**; *Vol. VIII:* **305**.

Suggested Instruments: *73 Annual:* "Sex-Role Stereotyping Rating Scale"; *79 Annual:* "Women as Managers Scale (WAMS)."

Lecturette Sources: *'77 Annual:* "Androgyny"; *79 Annual:* "Anybody with Eyes Can See the Facts!"

Submitted by Michael Maggio and Nancy Allen Good.

Notes on the Use of "All Iowans Are Naive":

ALL IOWANS ARE NAIVE CITY-AND-STATE COMBINATIONS

Spokane	Washington
Lubbock	Texas
Fresno	California
Wichita	Kansas
St. Petersburg	Florida

Bangor

Maine

Bismarck

North Dakota

Knoxville

Tennessee

Dayton

Ohio

Provo

Utah

ALL IOWANS ARE NAIVE REGIONAL STEREOTYPES

All West Virginians	are hillbillies.
All Californians	are dope addicts.
All Midwesterners	are provincial.
All New Yorkers	are snobs.
All Texans	are loud mouths.

All Oklahomans	are hicks.
All New Englanders	are brusque.
All Southerners	are bigots.
All Iowans	are naive.
All Floridians	are rich retirees.

ALL IOWANS ARE NAIVE OCCUPATIONAL STEREOTYPES

All artists	are temperamental.
All accountants	are dull and boring.
All lawyers	are unscrupulous.
All entertainers	are rich and shallow.
All psychiatrists	are crazy.

All politicians	are crooks.
All policemen	are "on the take."
All housewives	are unintelligent.
All used-car salesmen	are liars.
All truck drivers	are slovenly.

ALL IOWANS ARE NAIVE ETHNIC-GROUP STEREOTYPES

All blacks	are lazy.
All Arabs	are greedy.
All Orientals	are inscrutable.
All Italians	are members of the Mafia.
All Irish people	are heavy drinkers.

All Scottish people	are tight fisted.
All Puerto Ricans	are gang members.
All Polish people	are stupid.
All French people	are "on the make."
All English people	are aloof.

ALL IOWANS ARE NAIVE GENDER STEREOTYPES

All women	are bad drivers.
All women	are emotional.
All women	are illogical.
All women	are manipulative.
All women	are weak.

All men	are forgetful.
All men	are insensitive.
All men	are unemotional.
All men	are preoccupied with sex.
All men	are selfish.

345. CONSTRUCTIVE CRITICISM: RATING LEADERSHIP ABILITIES

Goals

I. To provide an opportunity for the members of an intact group to give and receive feedback regarding their leadership abilities.

II. To give the members experience in evaluating themselves and others in a constructive, concrete manner.

Group Size

All members of an intact group assembled into subgroups of four to six participants each.

Time Required

One and one-half to two hours.

Materials

I. Blank paper and a pencil for each participant.

II. A newsprint flip chart and a felt-tipped marker or a chalkboard and chalk.

Physical Setting

A room in which all groups can meet and work without disturbing one another. Writing surfaces should be provided for all participants.

Process

I. The facilitator briefly explains the activity and its goals and then delivers a lecturette on the following components of leadership: *flexibility, fairness, sensitivity to others, supportiveness, openness, decisiveness, knowledgeability, resourcefulness, judgment,* and *dedication.* As each of these components is presented, it is posted on newsprint or a chalkboard. (Fifteen minutes.)

II. The participants are assembled into groups of four to six each, and blank paper and pencils are distributed.

III. The members of each group are asked to work individually to rate their own leadership abilities as well as those of the other members. In order to do this, each participant refers to the posted list of components and rates himself or herself as well as every other group member on each component. The rating system is based on a scale of 1 to 5, where *1* represents the *lowest* demonstration of a given component and 5 represents the *highest*. (Twenty minutes.)

IV. The members of each group are instructed to share their ratings, concentrating on the leadership performance of one member at a time: The individual being focused on receives feedback from the other members and then shares his or her self-ratings; subsequently, the entire group discusses the similarities and differences between the self-assessments and the assessments made by the other members. (Forty-five minutes.)

V. The total group is reconvened, and the facilitator leads the processing of the activity by eliciting what the participants learned about leadership, themselves, and the process of giving and receiving feedback. (Twenty minutes.)

VI. After reassembling the individual groups, the facilitator asks each participant to select some way in which he or she would like to improve leadership performance and to discuss an improvement plan with fellow group members.

Variations

I. The individual groups may be asked to establish their own lists of leadership components and to evaluate one another on the basis of these components.

II. During Step III each group member may be asked to guess how the other members will rate him or her.

III. The activity may be altered so that only the group leader is rated.

IV. Expectations may be substituted for performance ratings. This use provides a way to set goals at the beginning of a workshop or training event and then to evaluate whether these goals were met.

V. Characteristics other than leadership ability may be evaluated.

Similar Structured Experiences: *Vol. I:* Structured Experiences **13, 17**; *Vol. II:* **38**; *Vol. III:* **57**; *Vol. IV:* **107**; *Vol. V:* **170**; *Vol. VI:* **209**; *'78 Annual:* **225**; *Vol. VIII:* **296, 303, 315**; *'82 Annual:* **326**.

Suggested Instruments: *'75 Annual:* "Group Leadership Functions Scale"; *'81 Annual:* "Patterns of Effective Supervisory Behavior"; *'83 Annual:* "The Team Orientation and Behavior Inventory (TOBI)."

Lecturette Sources: *73 Annual:* "The Johari Window: A Model for Soliciting and Giving Feedback"; *77 Annual:* "A Practical Leadership Paradigm."

Notes on the Use of "Constructive Criticism":

Submitted by Fred E. Woodall.

346. POWER CAUCUS: DEFINING AND NEGOTIATING

Goals

I. To help the participants to clarify their own definitions of power.

II. To allow the participants to experience the similarities and differences between these definitions and the application of power in a real situation.

Group Size

Three groups of three to six participants each.

Time Required

One hour and forty-five minutes.

Materials

I. Newsprint for each group.

II. A felt-tipped marker for each group.

III. Masking tape for each group.

Physical Setting

A room with a table and movable chairs for each group. The tables should be positioned in such a way that the participants can face the center of the room in Step IV.

Process

I. The participants are assembled into three groups and are told that each group is to prepare *a five-minute presentation that defines individual power in terms of verbal and nonverbal behavior.* The facilitator gives each group newsprint, a felt-tipped marker, and masking tape and states that these materials may be used, if desired, to create visual aids to accompany the presentation. In addition, the facilitator clarifies that the presentation may consist of a skit, an interview, or any other format that the members choose. Then the groups are informed that they have forty-five minutes to complete their task and are asked to begin.

II. When the allotted time has passed, the facilitator asks the groups to take turns making their presentations. (Fifteen minutes.)

III. After all presentations have been completed, the facilitator asks each group to caucus briefly to select its most influential member as a representative. It is explained that during the next step the three group representatives will meet in the center of the room to discuss, negotiate, and arrive at a consensus regarding which of the three definitions of power just presented is the most accurate. (Fifteen minutes.)

IV. The three group representatives move their chairs to the center of the room, form a circle, and carry out the task explained in the previous step. The remaining participants are instructed to listen to and observe the ways in which the representatives influence one another during the discussion.

V. After ten minutes the facilitator stops the representatives' conversation, reconvenes the total group, and leads a discussion of the entire activity. The following questions may be helpful during this discussion:

1. What seem to be the most significant verbal and nonverbal indicators of power? How were these indicators demonstrated in this activity? What was their impact?

2. On what basis was the most influential member of each group chosen? Did the group representatives behave as usual or differently when speaking together? If they behaved differently, what were the differences?

3. What feelings does power stimulate in you? How do you feel about your own power? about that of others?

4. In what ways do the final definition and the behaviors you just observed coincide with your own experience of power?

5. What have you learned about power that may be helpful to you in your back-home situation?

Variations

I. Additional participants may be accommodated by increasing the number of groups as well as the time allotted for Step IV.

II. During Step III the members of each group may be asked to use their definition of power as a basis for rating one another's influence and choosing the most influential member.

III. Process observers may be appointed and asked to report observations on the group representatives' behavior during Step IV.

IV. A final presentation (such as a skit or interview) may be developed by each group after the representatives have reached consensus.

Similar Structured Experiences: *Vol. III:* Structured Experience **59**; *Vol. IV:* **121**; *Vol. V:* **167**; *'77 Annual:* **195**; *Vol. VII:* **266**; *'80 Annual:* **277**.

Suggested Instruments: *'78 Annual:* "Mach V Attitude Inventory"; *'79 Annual:* "Power and OD Intervention Analysis (PODIA)."

Lecturette Source: *'76 Annual:* "Power."

Notes on the Use of "Power Caucus":

Submitted by Bradford F. Spencer.

347. ELM STREET COMMUNITY CHURCH: THIRD-PARTY CONSULTATION

Goals

I. To provide the participants with an experience that simulates collaborative problem solving within an organization.

II. To develop the participants' understanding of the role of a process consultant.

III. To build skills in diagnosing organizational and group problems.

Group Size

A maximum of three groups of nine to eleven participants each. (The role play calls for eight participants as church leaders and one participant as a process consultant; however, a group of ten or eleven participants can be accommodated by asking two or three members to form a team of consultants.) In order to complete the activity, the participants need to have some familiarity with the concept of organization development.

Time Required

Approximately three hours.

Materials

I. A copy of the Elm Street Community Church Background Sheet for each participant.

II. A set of Elm Street Community Church Role Sheets 1 through 8 for each group (a different sheet for each of eight members).

III. A copy of the Elm Street Community Church Additional-Information Sheet for each participant.

IV. Nine to eleven name tags for each group. Prior to conducting the activity, the facilitator completes these tags with the names and corresponding role functions appearing on the background sheet (eight tags with the characters' names plus one to three tags reading "Consultant").

V. A newsprint flip chart and a felt-tipped marker for each group.

VI. A roll of masking tape for each group.

VII. A copy of the Elm Street Community Church Observation Sheet for each participant who serves as a consultant.

VIII. A copy of the Elm Street Community Church Analysis Sheet for each participant consultant.

IX. A pencil for each participant consultant.

X. A clipboard or other portable writing surface for each participant consultant.

XI. A newsprint flip chart and a felt-tipped marker or a chalkboard and chalk (for the facilitator's use).

Physical Setting

A large room in which the groups can conduct their meetings without disturbing one another. Each group should be positioned near a wall so that sheets of newsprint can be displayed within the view of all of its members. In addition, a separate room should be provided for the purpose of briefing the participant consultants.

Process

I. The facilitator delivers a lecturette describing the interaction between content and process in terms of group and organizational outcomes. This lecturette should emphasize the following points:

1. The process by which a group resolves its problems is often as important as the solutions that are reached; and

2. A third-party consultant can facilitate this process by providing group members with feedback about their functioning and interaction, thereby assisting them in making the process more satisfying as well as more effective.

After completing the lecturette, the facilitator introduces the goals of the activity. (Fifteen minutes.)

II. Groups of nine to eleven participants each are formed, and copies of the Elm Street Community Church Background Sheet are distributed. After the participants have read the handout, those who are selected to act as consultants are asked to form a separate group in another room and to await instructions. Then the role sheets and name tags are given to the remaining members of each group in such a way that each member is assigned a different role. The players are asked to put on their name tags and to study their roles until the facilitator returns.

III. The facilitator meets with the group of participant consultants and distributes name tags, copies of the observation sheet and the analysis sheet, pencils, and clipboards or other portable writing surfaces. Then the consultants are asked to put on their name tags and are briefed on their role in diagnosis and intervention. During this briefing the use of the handouts is explained: The observation sheet is to be completed while the group is working independently without the assistance of the consultant, and the analysis sheet provides questions that the consultant should ask while facilitating the meeting and helping the group to resolve its difficulties. After it has been determined that the consulting function is clearly understood, the consultants are invited to return with the facilitator to the main assembly room. (Ten minutes.)

IV.   The facilitator elicits questions, clarifies the role-play situation as necessary, emphasizes the need for authentic role behavior to simulate reality, and instructs the groups to begin.

V.   The facilitator monitors the group meetings and allows each to continue for twenty minutes. At this point the members of each group are given copies of the Elm Street Community Church Additional-Information Sheet. After reading this sheet, they continue the role play, using the information provided.

VI.   After another twenty minutes the meetings are stopped, but the participants are cautioned to maintain their roles. Each group's consultant is instructed to give feedback to the role players about the group dynamics that he or she observed. Subsequently, the consultant leads a discussion of this feedback, and the church members decide how they want to use it. The entire feedback phase is allowed to continue for twenty minutes; then each meeting is resumed.

VII.   After forty-five minutes each participant consultant is asked to facilitate the rest of the meeting, helping the members to address appropriate issues and to resolve their problems. (The consultant is given a newsprint flip chart, a felt-tipped marker, and a roll of masking tape so that the group's ideas can be recorded and posted.)

VIII.   After thirty more minutes the role plays are stopped. The facilitator writes the following questions on newsprint or a chalkboard and instructs the members of each group to discuss them.

1.   What became the real issue for you?

2.   How satisfied were you with the process? Did your level of satisfaction change as a result of the feedback and assistance provided by the consultant? If so, how?

3.   What comments would you like to address to the consultant regarding his or her behavior? Which specific behaviors were helpful? Which were not?

(Fifteen minutes.)

IX.   The facilitator leads the total group in summarizing helpful approaches to diagnosing group and organizational problems.

Variations

I. The members of each group may be given additional time to complete the task, and the consultant may be instructed to provide feedback periodically regarding observations.

II. The participant consultants may be instructed to use different types of interventions (see '72 *Annual*, "Seven Pure Strategies of Change").

III. One group may be asked to operate without a consultant; after the role plays are stopped, the functioning of this group is compared with that of the consultant-assisted group(s).

IV. After Step IX the participants who are experiencing similar problems back home may receive assistance from fellow group members in diagnosing their problems.

Similar Structured Experiences: *Vol. III:* Structured Experience **73**; *Vol. IV:* **111**; '74 *Annual:* **126, 131**; '75 *Annual:* **139**; '77 *Annual:* **193**; *Vol. VI:* **200, 211**; '78 *Annual:* **230**; '83 *Annual:* **337**.

Suggested Instruments: '75 *Annual:* "Problem-Analysis Questionnaire"; '78 *Annual:* "Critical Consulting Incidents Inventory (CCII)"; '81 *Annual:* "Organizational-Process Survey."

Lecturette Sources: '77 *Annual:* "Constructive Conflict in Discussions: Learning to Manage Disagreements Effectively"; '80 *Annual:* "A Nine-Step Problem-Solving Model"; '83 *Annual:* "A Guide to Problem Solving."

Notes on the Use of "Elm Street Community Church":

Submitted by Charles E. List.

ELM STREET COMMUNITY CHURCH BACKGROUND SHEET

The Elm Street Community Church was founded in 1947. It started with four families and over the years grew in size to a congregation of 680 at its peak, at which time a new church structure was completed to accommodate a wide variety of activities.

Reverend Dale has been the church's only minister except for Chris, who was ordained as the assistant pastor five years ago. Pastor Chris is twenty-six years old and holds very progressive, liberal views of theology, whereas Reverend Dale holds traditional and conservative attitudes toward the role of the church in its ministry to the community it serves.

The congregation has been declining progressively from 680 members six years ago to 460 at present. Because contributions have dropped proportionately, it is difficult to make ends meet; the church not only holds a $145,000 mortgage, but also must pay the expenses for running the many programs it conducts on a regular basis.

Reverend Dale has called a meeting of all the church leaders to discuss the declining membership and the budget deficit. In addition to *Reverend Dale* and *Pastor Chris*, the following leaders are present: *Lee, the director of youth education; Terry, the Sunday school superintendent; Kelly, the choirmaster; Pat, the financial manager; Sandy, the church-council president;* and *Lynn, the president of the Ladies' Aid Society.* Also in attendance are one or more process consultants who will try to help the leaders as they work on resolving their predicament.

At the outset Reverend Dale specifies that by the end of the meeting the group must have arrived at ways to deal with the membership and money difficulties.

ELM STREET COMMUNITY CHURCH ROLE SHEET 1

Reverend Dale

You feel that the church's problems are attributable to the liberal innovations instituted over the past five years. Examples are the rock-and-roll service established by Pastor Chris and the religious blues music that Kelly likes to have the choir perform.

You also believe that Sandy, the president of the church council, is not only too tolerant of these unorthodox activities, but also too lax about member commitment. For example, Sandy vehemently opposed you when you began enforcing the 10-percent pledge requirement four years ago. As far as you are concerned, the members of the congregation must live up to their financial obligation to the church, and you are not afraid to tell them so in your sermons. You have even had Pat, the financial manager, phone or visit those who fail to maintain their pledges. To you this approach is warranted as part of the trend toward fundamentalism that you hope to revive.

Do not show this role description to anyone.

ELM STREET COMMUNITY CHURCH ROLE SHEET 2

Pastor Chris

Since assuming your position as *assistant pastor*, you have argued continually with Reverend Dale about the direction that the church should pursue in order to have wider appeal in the community. The problem lies in Reverend Dale's fundamentalist attitude. For instance, the 10-percent pledge about which the Reverend is so adamant is outdated; it should be de-emphasized, and the heavy-handed methods of collecting it from the members should be eliminated.

Essentially, you support an approach based less on the Bible and more on social issues. You are a firm believer that the church is part of the community and as such should serve a broad range of individual beliefs. For this reason you are a strong supporter of Lynn, the president of the Ladies' Aid Society, who wants to start an assertiveness-training program for the women in the church. You are also interested in future programs on subjects such as self-hypnosis and sexual enrichment for couples. The innovations you have already tried would have been successful if the Reverend had not openly expressed negative feelings toward them.

You feel that it is time for Reverend Dale to retire.

Do not show this role description to anyone.

ELM STREET COMMUNITY CHURCH ROLE SHEET 3

Lee

You are very conservative, and you take your position as *director of youth education* very seriously. The problem that is of paramount concern to you is that the young people in the congregation are participating in activities that will jeopardize their religious upbringing. For example, in your absence the teenagers spend their time in the recreation room dancing and smoking and doing who knows what else. You have heard about this situation from several boys and girls whose parents will not allow them to attend events at the church anymore. In your opinion the church council should fire Pastor Chris, who is responsible for the trouble, and then seek to affiliate with a fundamentalist denomination that will not tolerate liberal activities.

As far as the monetary issue is concerned, you feel that a 10-percent pledge is too much to ask of people and that it should no longer be enforced.

Do not show this role description to anyone.

ELM STREET COMMUNITY CHURCH ROLE SHEET 4

Terry

As the *Sunday school superintendent*, you would like to see the children read only the Bible and discontinue the use of the religious materials that have been part of the curriculum for the past few years. These materials were recommended by Lynn and the Ladies' Aid Society, and, although they were approved for purchase by the church council, you feel that they are too liberal in content.

Also, you would like to continue the pledge requirement of three dollars per child per month. This requirement teaches the children to give unselfishly at an early age, and this practice will carry over into adulthood.

Do not show this role description to anyone.

ELM STREET COMMUNITY CHURCH ROLE SHEET 5

Kelly

You have been the *choirmaster* for the past five years. Before you assumed your position, all the hymns sung in church were very slow in tempo and restrained in emotional content. However, you have introduced a wide variety of contemporary religious and some nonreligious music into the services.

You know that Reverend Dale does not like such music and favors returning to the old repertoire. In addition, you believe that Lee is encouraging the teenagers not to sing in the choir, but to start their own choral group instead and sing only basic hymns. Pastor Chris, on the other hand, seems pleased with your selections.

You would like to see Lee replaced as director of youth education because you feel that he is driving people away from the church.

Do not show this role description to anyone.

ELM STREET COMMUNITY CHURCH ROLE SHEET 6

Pat

You are the church's *financial manager*. In terms of philosophy, you are an extreme traditionalist. You have always pledged 10 percent of your earnings to the church because you feel that God demands it. As far as you are concerned, the church has been weakened over the past ten years by new members who strongly oppose tithing.

To you there is an obvious solution to the money problems: The congregation should be composed only of those who are willing to give as much money as it takes to run the church; the others should go elsewhere. It also seems that if some of the programs were eliminated, two pastors would not be needed. Paying one salary instead of two would save a lot of money right away.

Do not show this role description to anyone.

ELM STREET COMMUNITY CHURCH ROLE SHEET 7

Sandy

You are a moderate who was elected *president of the church council* as a compromise candidate. In your opinion the church should offer programs that serve a broad range of beliefs.

It is apparent to you that the immediate situation is evolving toward a win-lose power struggle. Consequently, because you would like to see the parties involved avoid open conflict, you decide to act as a harmonizer and compromiser during the meeting.

Do not show this role description to anyone.

ELM STREET COMMUNITY CHURCH ROLE SHEET 8

Lynn

You are a strong advocate of women's rights. In addition to serving as the *president of the Ladies' Aid Society,* you are active in several organizations that support the women's movement. In your opinion the women in the church need to be shaken out of their complacency. Although many of them share your views, they are hesitant to express these views as readily as you do. Reverend Dale's wife, for example, has a latent desire to be more liberated but is dominated by her husband; she attends the society's meetings against his will.

Consequently, you want to start an assertiveness-training program within the church. Pastor Chris plans to support you in this endeavor as well as in your attempts to make the Ladies' Aid Society more relevant in today's world. The members of the society, like you, are anxious to do more than just raise money for the church. You find such limited responsibilities not only demeaning, but also repressive to the emerging role of contemporary women.

During the meeting you intend to make your views clear.

Do not show this role description to anyone.

ELM STREET COMMUNITY CHURCH
ADDITIONAL-INFORMATION SHEET

All of the 220 members who have left Elm Street Community Church over the last six years were asked to complete questionnaires that dealt with their feelings about the church, their reasons for leaving, and their patterns of contributing. Of this number, 175 returned completed questionnaires. Some of their responses are categorized and listed as follows.

Reasons for Leaving

Number of Respondents	*Reason Cited*
105	Joined another church affiliated with a denomination and a clearly established religious philosophy
75	Felt that they were too conservative for the church
30	Felt that they were too liberal for the church
30	No longer wished to attend any church
20	Were upset with the conflict of philosophies within the church
10	Joined a cult
5	No longer felt socially oriented enough to be members
5	"Joined" a conservative radio ministry

Note: A number of people cited more than one reason.

Average Weekly Contributions

Percentage of Respondents	*Amount*
40	$25 or more
35	$10 or more
15	$ 5 or more
5	$ 1 or more
5	(did not give on a weekly basis)

Note: At present the average weekly contribution per member is $4.

In addition, twenty-five of the 175 people who completed and returned question-naires were interviewed. When asked individually to give their main reasons for leaving, the results were as follows:

Number of Respondents	*Reason Cited*
12	Felt that the church did not espouse any particular beliefs
8	Felt that new members did not carry their fair share of the financial responsibilities
3	Felt that the church was no longer conservative
2	Felt that the church was not liberal enough

ELM STREET COMMUNITY CHURCH OBSERVATION SHEET

As you observe the meeting, make notes on the following subjects. Later you will be asked to brief the members on your observations.

Main Problem Area (as interpreted by the group)

1. Clarity of definition of the main problem:

2. Causes of the problem:

3. Underlying issues:

4. Different views of the problem:

5. Tentative solutions offered:

6. Unknown data needed to understand the problem and to develop solutions:

Group Process

1. Task effectiveness (progress toward objective of meeting):

2. Attention to group maintenance:

3. Communication effectiveness:

4. Decision-making pattern:

5. Openness:

6. Energy level:

ELM STREET COMMUNITY CHURCH ANALYSIS SHEET

Ask the group members the following questions and list their responses on newsprint. *Do not become involved in the content of the discussion; facilitate the process.* As you fill each sheet of newsprint, tape it to the wall in view of the entire group.

1. What must be done before attempting to resolve the main problem?
2. What is the clearest statement of the main problem?
3. What are the major issues that are related to the problem?
4. What must be changed in order to resolve the problem?
5. What are some alternative approaches to making the necessary changes?
6. What criteria should be used to evaluate these approaches?
7. On the basis of these criteria, what approaches can be agreed on as solutions?

348. INQUIRIES:
OBSERVING AND BUILDING HYPOTHESES

Goals

I. To provide the participants with experience in discovering relationships and meanings in an unfamiliar situation.

II. To help the participants to become aware of their own methods of observing, gathering data, and building hypotheses.

III. To allow the participants an opportunity to test the validity of these methods.

Group Size

Twelve to sixteen participants.

Time Required

Approximately two hours.

Materials

I. One copy of the appropriate Inquiries Role Description for each of the four role players (Participants A, B, C, and D).

II. One copy of the Inquiries Scientific Team Directions for each member of this team.

III. One copy of the Inquiries Investigating Team Directions for each member of this team.

IV. A pencil for each scientist and each investigator.

V. A clipboard or other portable writing surface for each scientist and each investigator.

VI. Masking tape.

VII. Ten pennies.

VIII. Ten dimes.

IX. One soup can.

Physical Setting

A room with enough space so that the participants can move around freely. This activity involves a simple mechanical process that is carried out by four participants who are designated as Participant A, Participant B, Participant C, and Participant D. Two tables, several chairs, and an arrow constructed of masking tape adhering to the floor are needed for this process. The following diagram illustrates the room arrangement required, including the starting positions for Participants A, B, C, and D and the placement of chairs for the scientists and the investigators.

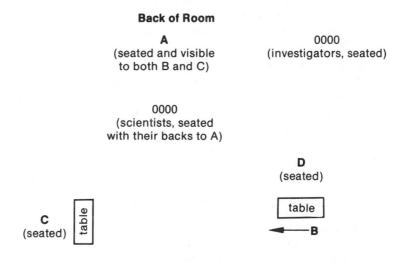

Back of Room

A
(seated and visible
to both B and C)

0000
(investigators, seated)

0000
(scientists, seated
with their backs to A)

D
(seated)

table

C
(seated)   table

◄——— **B**

Front of Room

The ten pennies and ten dimes are placed on the table between Participants B and D, and the soup can is placed on the table behind which Participant C is seated.

Process

I. The facilitator begins by asking for volunteers and choosing four participants to serve as A, B, C, and D. Each is given his or her respective role sheet and is asked to read and study the sheet.

II. Four more participants are selected as members of the scientific team and are taken outside the room. The remaining participants are invited to talk quietly among themselves until the facilitator returns, but Participants A, B, C, and D are cautioned against discussing their role sheets. Each scientist is given a copy of the Inquiries Scientific Team Directions, a pencil, and a clipboard or other portable writing surface. The scientists are asked to read their directions and to prepare for the activity until the facilitator invites them to rejoin the others. If any questions are asked about the "rules" or the specifics of the activity, the facilitator reiterates, "Read your directions." Then the facilitator returns to the room.

III. Those participants who have not yet been assigned a function are designated as members of the investigating team and are escorted to chairs at the back of the room. Each investigator is given a copy of the Inquiries Investigating Team Directions, a pencil, and a clipboard or other portable writing surface and is asked to read the directions. The facilitator clarifies that while the investigators are waiting for the scientists to return, they may observe the activity in the room and quietly discuss the situation among themselves.

IV. Participant A is identified for Participants B and C. Then Participants A, B, C, and D are escorted to their starting positions. The facilitator requests that they begin the actions described in their handouts and continue until told to stop. None of these participants is allowed clarification of any role except his or her own, and such clarification is given only after the actions have begun.

V. When the scientists have been out of the room for fifteen minutes, the facilitator invites them to return, escorts them to their chairs, and asks them to begin their task. The activity continues for twenty minutes. During this time the facilitator monitors what is happening, but refuses to answer any questions.

VI. The facilitator stops the activity, instructs the team of scientists to sit in a circle in the center of the room, and asks the remaining participants to move closer to the scientists so that they can hear. One member of the scientific team is asked to read the team's directions to the total group, and then all members are instructed to discuss their findings while the remaining participants listen and observe. After five minutes the scientists are asked to appoint a spokesperson, who then reports their conclusions to the total group. (Fifteen minutes.)

VII. The investigators are instructed to replace the scientists in the center of the room and to repeat the procedure of Step VI. (Fifteen minutes.)

VIII. The facilitator invites the scientists and the investigators to share their feelings about the activity. (Ten minutes.)

IX. Participants A, B, C, and D are asked to take turns reading their role descriptions and then are invited to share their feelings about the activity. (Ten minutes.)

X. Using the following questions as a guide, the facilitator leads a discussion of the entire experience.

1. Did you assume any "rules" that had not been stipulated? If so, what were they?

2. How did your preconceptions affect your conclusions?

3. How did the various methods for reaching conclusions differ? Which were effective? Which were ineffective?

4. How do these methods compare with the way you usually operate in reaching conclusions and testing them?

5. Did the spokespersons' reports accurately reflect their groups' conclusions?

6. How did reactions to the experience differ among the participants, the scientists, and the investigators? How do you account for these differences?

7. How might you relate this experience to your back-home situation?

Variations

I. A group of omniscient observers may be added.

II. If the scientists' initial conclusions are incorrect, they may be allowed to receive clues or to meet together to discuss the situation. Subsequently, they resume their task.

Similar Structured Experiences: *Vol. IV:* Structured Experience **111**; *74 Annual:* **131**; *77 Annual:* **193**; *Vol. VI:* **213**.

Lecturette Source: *79 Annual:* "Anybody with Eyes Can See the Facts!"

Notes on the Use of "Inquiries":

Submitted by Steven E. Aufrecht.

INQUIRIES SCIENTIFIC TEAM DIRECTIONS

You are a member of a team of scientists. This team is seeking a grant from the National Science Foundation to study the problems of minority patients in public hospitals. Before awarding the grant, the foundation wants to test the members' scientific abilities. The test that has been devised involves this task: *When you re-enter the room that you just left, find out what is happening in that room.*

You and your fellow team members have ten minutes to prepare yourselves for this task in any way that you see fit. After you are asked to re-enter the room, you will have twenty minutes before you are asked to discuss your findings and reach a conclusion.

INQUIRIES INVESTIGATING TEAM DIRECTIONS

You are a member of a team of investigators. The group that just left the room is a team of scientists. When the scientists return, they will attempt to find out what is happening in the room. Your task is to observe them in order to *discover how scientists work*. You will have twenty minutes to observe before you are asked to discuss your findings and reach a conclusion.

INQUIRIES ROLE DESCRIPTION

Participant A

During this activity you are to sit in an assigned spot and touch your left or right ear at least once every two minutes, but not more often than once in thirty seconds.

If you are asked any questions, you may answer them, but you need not tell the truth. *Do not show these directions to anyone.*

INQUIRIES ROLE DESCRIPTION

Participant B

During this activity you are to function as a *robot*. To assume your "ready" position, go to the tape arrow on the floor, face the direction of the arrowhead, and stand with one foot on each side of the arrow shaft. When the activity begins, you are to follow these directions explicitly and carefully:

1. Assume the "ready" position. When Participant A touches his or her *left ear*, mentally count to 10 and then take a *penny* from the pile of coins on the table situated to the right of the arrow. Walk in the direction of the arrow until you reach a person seated at a table with a soup can on it; this person will be positioned with one arm extended, hand held palm up. Drop the penny into the extended hand. Then reassume the "ready" position.

2. When Participant A touches his or her *right ear*, you are to follow the procedure outlined in Step 1, except that you are to use a *dime* instead of a penny.

3. If some obstacle is placed in your path, return to the "ready" position until that obstacle has been removed.

4. If the conditions are not exactly as specified in either Step 1 or Step 2, you must remain in the "ready" position. (For example, if the person to whom you are to deliver the coin is standing rather than sitting or has both hands extended rather than one, you may not move.)

5. If you are asked a question that can be answered with "yes" or "no" and you know the answer, you may respond. If you do not know the answer to such a question, say "yes-no." If the question cannot be answered with "yes" or "no"—regardless of whether you know the answer—respond with "maybe."

6. Do not react to any signals or instructions except those from Participant A. If someone tries to move you physically, do not resist; however, as soon as you are free, return to the "ready" position.

7. If another arrow is added to the floor, ignore it unless your "ready" arrow has been removed. In the absence of your "ready" arrow, go to the new one (or to the nearest, if more than one has been added) and make that your new "ready" position.

8. You may consult this sheet whenever necessary, but *do not show it to anyone.*

INQUIRIES ROLE DESCRIPTION

Participant C

During this activity you are to function as a *robot*. To assume your "ready" position, sit at the table with the soup can on it and fold your arms. When the activity begins, you are to follow these directions explicitly and carefully:

1. Assume the "ready" position. When Participant A touches his or her *left ear*, immediately extend your *left arm* in front of you and hold your hand with the palm up.

2. When Participant A touches his or her *right ear*, immediately extend your *right* arm in front of you and hold your hand with the palm up.

3. When a coin is placed in either hand, drop it into the soup can and reassume the "ready" position.

4. If you are asked a question that can be answered with "yes" or "no" and you know the answer, you may respond. If you do not know the answer to such a question, say "yes-no." If the question cannot be answered with "yes" or "no"—regardless of whether you know the answer—respond with "maybe."

5. Do not react to any signals or instructions except those from Participant A. If someone tries to move you physically, do not resist; however, as soon as you are free, return to the "ready" position.

6. You may consult this sheet whenever necessary, but *do not show it to anyone.*

INQUIRIES ROLE DESCRIPTION

Participant D

During this activity you are to sit in an assigned position beside a table. On this table are a number of pennies and dimes. Whenever this supply of coins dwindles so that there are only a few left, your task is to replenish the supply by following this procedure:

1. Walk to the table across the room;
2. Pick up the soup can;
3. Bring it back to your own area;
4. Empty the coins it contains onto your table;
5. Return the can; and
6. Reassume your original position.

You may answer any question that you are asked, but *do not show these directions to anyone.*

349. PERSONALITY TRAITS: SELF-DISCOVERY AND DISCLOSURE

Goals

I. To assist the participants in gaining insight about themselves.

II. To facilitate self-disclosure.

Group Size

Eight to twenty-four participants.

Time Required

Approximately one hour.

Materials

I. A copy of the Personality Traits Inventory for each participant.

II. A copy of the Personality Traits Scoring and Interpretation Sheet for each participant.

III. A pencil for each participant.

Physical Setting

A room in which the participants can work comfortably as a total group, in small groups, and in dyads. Writing surfaces are helpful but not essential.

Process

I. The facilitator distributes copies of the Personality Traits Inventory and pencils and instructs the participants to complete the instrument. (Ten minutes.)

II. Each participant is given a copy of the Personality Traits Scoring and Interpretation Sheet and is asked to read the interpretative material and to follow the instructions. Any necessary clarification is provided. (Ten minutes.)

III. The participants are assembled into groups of four to six each. The members of each group take turns sharing their results by describing themselves in terms of the instrument. (Fifteen minutes.)

IV. The facilitator asks the groups to divide into dyads to share the impact of the learnings derived from the instrument results. Each participant is also encouraged to discuss with his or her partner one or two areas of personal behavior that appear to be significant. (Fifteen minutes.)

V. The total group is reconvened, and the facilitator leads a discussion of the entire activity. Any or all of the following questions may be asked during this discussion:

1. What were the surprises?
2. Which preconceptions were reinforced?
3. What are your reactions to your personality as assessed by the instrument?
4. What are some differences between your personality in this environment and your personality in your work environment? What are the similarities?
5. What did you learn about yourself that might be helpful to you?

Variations

I. Group members may be asked to complete the instrument for one another rather than for themselves; in this case the activity focuses on the perceptions of others rather than self-perceptions.

II. The facilitator may use the instrument as a tool to measure changes during and after some type of intervention.

III. The instrument may be used in couples-awareness training.

Similar Structured Experiences: *Vol. I:* Structured Experience **13**; *'78 Annual:* **226**.

Suggested Instruments: *76 Annual:* "Inventory of Self-Actualizing Characteristics (ISAC)"; *77 Annual:* "Interpersonal Check List (ICL)"; *'80 Annual:* "Personal Style Inventory"; *'82 Annual:* "Life-Style Questionnaire."

Lecturette Sources: *73 Annual:* "Johari Window"; *78 Annual:* "Tolerance of Equivocality: The Bronco, Easy Rider, Blockbuster, and Nomad"; *'80 Annual:* "The Four-Communication-Styles Approach."

Submitted by William J. Schiller.

Notes on the Use of "Personality Traits":

PERSONALITY TRAITS INVENTORY

Indicate the frequency with which each of the following statements pertains to you by writing the appropriate response number in the corresponding blank.

Frequency Scale

1—Never

2—Infrequently

3—Sometimes

4—Often

5—Always

_____ 1. I have feelings of guilt and inferiority.

_____ 2. I am socially competent.

_____ 3. I welcome and look for challenges and variety.

_____ 4. I put things together in new or unusual ways.

_____ 5. I supervise or command.

_____ 6. I enjoy being the center of attention.

_____ 7. I show affection for others.

_____ 8. I de-emphasize or disregard external authority or control.

_____ 9. I punish myself.

_____ 10. I question my own worth.

_____ 11. I am able to obtain aid, service, assistance, or cooperation from others.

_____ 12. I am mentally capable in a variety of areas.

The characteristics dealt with in this instrument were selected from a number of personality descriptors presented in *A Manual for the Client's Self-Concept Instrument* by Lemire and Edgar, 1978. Lemire and Edgar chose their descriptors from several dozen commonly used personality tests and their accompanying technical manuals.

_____ 13. I am creative and original.

_____ 14. I am competitive.

_____ 15. I like to attract notice.

_____ 16. I do things for and with others.

_____ 17. I emphasize personal choice and freedom.

_____ 18. I tend to feel guilty and to express my guilt.

_____ 19. I am assertive.

_____ 20. I enjoy variety in personal and professional endeavors.

_____ 21. I am manipulative.

_____ 22. I direct my own life and actions.

_____ 23. I see others as rivals rather than potential friends or associates.

_____ 24. I treat others with kindness and understanding.

_____ 25. I quickly perceive another's thoughts and the relations between these thoughts.

_____ 26. I need to have a sense of belonging.

PERSONALITY TRAITS SCORING AND INTERPRETATION SHEET

The Personality Traits Inventory consists of twenty-six statements that are descriptive of various human characteristics. The respondent is asked to indicate, on a scale of one to five, how frequently each statement applies to himself or herself. Buried within these statements are eight separate personality traits. Final scoring results in a measure of the degree to which each trait describes the person in question.

To determine your scores for the eight traits, write your responses for the appropriate item numbers in the spaces provided below. Add your responses for each trait and divide by the number provided. The resulting number is your score for that particular trait. A score of 5 means that the trait is highly descriptive of you, whereas a score of 1 means that the trait is not at all descriptive of you.

Tendency to Feel Inferior (low sense of self-worth)

1._____

9._____

10._____

18._____

TOTAL_____   ÷ 4 = _____

Social Competence (ability to be at ease with, to cooperate with, and to gain cooperation from others)

2._____

11._____

19._____

TOTAL_____   ÷ 3 = _____

Preference for Variety (eagerness for new or different endeavors; ability to adjust easily to change)

3._____

12._____

20._____

TOTAL_____ ÷ 3 = _____

Creativity (originality in thoughts and actions; ability to rearrange existing things into new patterns)

4._____

13._____

TOTAL_____ ÷ 2 = _____

Desire to Dominate (tendency to compete, to view others as rivals, to manipulate, and to assume control of situations)

5._____

14._____

21._____

23._____

TOTAL_____ ÷ 4 = _____

Exhibition (desire to attract notice and to be the center of attention)

6._____

15._____

TOTAL_____ ÷ 2 = _____

Affiliation (need to feel a sense of belonging, to do things for and with others, and to be kind)

7._____

16._____

24._____

26._____

TOTAL_____ ÷ 4 = _____

Autonomy (tendency to direct own life and actions, to exercise personal choice and freedom, and to disregard external authority and control)

8._____

17._____

22._____

25._____

TOTAL_____ ÷ 4 = _____

350. DEPARTMENTAL DILEMMA: SHARED DECISION MAKING

Goals

I. To increase the participants' awareness of the process and skills involved in shared decision making.

II. To allow the participants to experience shared decision making as a means of conflict management.

Group Size

An unlimited number of groups of eight participants each.

Time Required

Approximately three hours.

Materials

I. A copy of the Departmental Dilemma Case-Study Sheet for each participant.

II. One set of Departmental Dilemma Role Sheets 1 through 8 for each group (a different role sheet for each member of each group).

III. A newsprint flip chart and a felt-tipped marker or a chalkboard and chalk.

IV. Blank paper and a pencil for each spokesperson.

V. A clipboard or other portable writing surface for each spokesperson.

Physical Setting

A large room in which the individual groups can work without disturbing one another. If the facilitator wishes to encourage a more independent approach to learning or is not able to observe all groups at all times, each group may complete Step II on its own in a setting of its choice.

Process

I. The facilitator forms groups of eight participants each. Copies of the Departmental Dilemma Case-Study Sheet are distributed, and it is explained that each group will be meeting to deal with the problem inherent in the case study. After the participants have read the handout, the facilitator distributes copies of the role sheets, ensuring that each member of each group is given a different sheet. Then the participants are asked to study their roles. (Fifteen minutes.)

II. The facilitator writes the following questions on newsprint or a chalkboard, explaining that these questions are to form the basis of the upcoming meetings.

1. How do the various members feel about shared decision making? What are its advantages? its drawbacks?

2. How has the issue of shared decision making affected the department?

3. What conflicts are being experienced by the members?

4. What can be done to resolve these conflicts?

5. How might the conflicts have been avoided?

Each group is instructed to answer these questions and to select a spokesperson to record answers and to report them later to the total group. Blank paper, a pencil, and a clipboard or other portable writing surface are given to each group for the spokesperson's use. In addition, the facilitator emphasizes that each participant must maintain his or her assigned role while completing this task. Then the groups are informed that their time limit is one hour and are asked to begin the role play.

III. After the hour has passed, the facilitator stops the role plays and reconvenes the entire group. The spokespersons are invited to share the results of the previous step. Then the facilitator leads a total-group discussion by asking the following questions:

1. What were your feelings while playing your role? What did you want to do?

2. How did you react to the other roles? How did you want to change them?

3. What would you predict as the future for Department X if nothing changes?

4. How can you apply the experiences of Department X to your back-home situation?

(Forty minutes.)

IV. The participants are asked to reassemble into their groups and to build on what they have learned in order to develop principles of shared decision making. The facilitator specifies that these principles should be ones that allow shared decision making to be an ongoing process. The spokespersons are instructed to record these principles so that they can be shared later with the total group. (Twenty minutes.)

V. The total group is reconvened, and the spokespersons are asked to share the principles recommended by their groups. Then the facilitator leads a discussion on the effectiveness of these principles.

Variations

I. In Step II one group may enact the role play for the remaining participants, who act as observers.

II. During Step III the facilitator may instruct the members of each group to reach a consensus regarding the conflicts inherent in the case and to write a group report in which they outline their recommendations and implementation strategy. After all reports have been completed, the facilitator asks the groups to share their experiences while working on this task and to explain the contributions made by each member.

III. Issues involving leadership may be emphasized.

Similar Structured Experiences: *Vol. I:* Structured Experience **11**; *Vol. II:* **41**; *Vol. III:* **67**; *'74 Annual:* **132**; *'75 Annual:* **141**; *Vol. V:* **151**, **154**; *'77 Annual:* **186**, **187**; *Vol. VI:* **207**; *'78 Annual:* **223**.

Suggested Instruments: *73 Annual:* "LEAD (Leadership: Employee-Orientation and Differentiation) Questionnaire"; *'81 Annual:* "Diagnosing Organizational Conflict-Management Climates."

Lecturette Sources: *73 Annual:* "Synergy and Consensus-Seeking"; *74 Annual:* "Conflict-Resolution Strategies"; *75 Annual:* "Participatory Management: A New Morality," "Open Systems"; *77 Annual:* "Handling Group and Organizational Conflict"; *79 Annual:* "Encouraging Others to Change Their Behavior"; *'81 Annual:* "Defensive and Supportive Communication."

Notes on the Use of "Departmental Dilemma":

Submitted by Janet H. Stevenson.

DEPARTMENTAL DILEMMA CASE STUDY SHEET

Medway Research Associates is a company funded by government to conduct research in a variety of areas. There are many departments in the company, with seven to fifty members in each. Most of these departments function in a participative, democratic fashion. Members in a department decide what role the chairperson will play and what his or her duties and those of committees within the department will be. Such duties are referred to as "operating procedures" and are approved by each department in a meeting attended by all members. Approval is granted by majority vote, and all members, including the chairperson, have equal input. In addition, there are regular meetings at which matters concerning the department are presented and discussed.

The problem at hand concerns Department X, which has no formal operating procedures. The chairperson of Department X, Randall Todd, is in the third year of a five-year contract for his position. During this term Randall has introduced many good changes, some of which incorporated the input of other department members and some of which he simply announced.

When Randall first became chairperson, he told his department that his policy would be to make all decisions himself until the researchers indicated a willingness to participate in the decision-making process. However, he made it clear that he was interested in member participation and that he did not want "yes men" on his research team. He also declared that he had an open-door policy concerning complaints and suggestions, but that he preferred to deal with people on an individual basis rather than in meetings. In addition, he encouraged the researchers to pursue avenues of personal and professional development.

Although Randall has made it clear that he will call a department meeting whenever anyone wants him to do so, thus far meetings have been held only for the presentation or discussion of important issues. There is little participation at these meetings; many members have tried to participate, but their ideas have been glossed over when Randall has not liked them.

Elizabeth, one of the researchers, has worked closely with Randall in the past three years. Randall has used the ideas she has generated and has been publicly appreciative of her contributions. Elizabeth has been the opposite of a "yes man," feeling free to generate discussion, suggestions, and criticisms. Recently Randall publicly expressed the wish that others would follow suit. At that time Elizabeth suggested a department meeting to discuss the possibility of instituting shared decision making as a standard policy. Randall became defensive and rather antagonistic when presented with this request, but finally acceded.

The meeting is to take place in a few minutes.

DEPARTMENTAL DILEMMA ROLE SHEET 1

Randall

For three years you have worked very hard as chairperson of your department. You like to control; essentially, you disdain the administrative pattern of other departments and prefer to work with your researchers on a one-to-one basis. Although you are basically a pleasant person and are concerned about the progress of department meetings, you are rather nervous and lacking in social ease; consequently, you communicate only what you feel is necessary for the employees to know, and you are often seen as brusque.

You are aware that your policies and behavior may seem contradictory to the researchers, but you want to avoid discussing this contradiction if the subject arises during the upcoming meeting.

Do not show this role sheet to anyone.

DEPARTMENTAL DILEMMA ROLE SHEET 2

Elizabeth

Not only are you a good worker and experienced in your job; you are also helpful, fair minded, and interested in sharing the work load. You have good ideas and are willing to stand up for your beliefs both privately and publicly. Furthermore, you are friendly and you have a high concern for people generally and especially for those in your department. You want the department to develop in a positive way, and you are interested in shared decision making as a means for accomplishing this development.

Your fellow department members frequently tell you that they wish Randall were as receptive to their ideas as he is to your own. You plan to broach this subject in the meeting, despite your concern that Randall may see you as disruptive for doing so. In fact, you intend to hold him to his word about welcoming shared decision making.

Do not show this role sheet to anyone.

DEPARTMENTAL DILEMMA ROLE SHEET 3

Chris

You have been a Medway employee longer than anyone else in the department, and you have a permanent contract with the company. You are friendly, well liked, and a good worker.

You have accepted many changes in the past few years in the department, some willingly and others unwillingly. Although you are vocal with your fellow researchers and frequently express complaints in private, "let-off-steam" sessions, you are not this way when Randall is present; in fact, you rarely speak at department meetings. In essence, you are not interested in shared decision making if it involves more work or any confrontation; you simply want to do your job and go home.

You are hoping that the upcoming meeting is short and free from tension.

Do not show this role sheet to anyone.

DEPARTMENTAL DILEMMA ROLE SHEET 4

Lee

You have a permanent contract with Medway. You are fair minded, pleasant, and a good worker.

You have been very quiet until recently, when you have become more vocal with your fellow researchers. Although some of the other department members have encouraged you to stand up to Randall, you are neither willing nor able to do so. When the crunch comes, you always back down; you cannot stand the pressure of departmental unrest and will do anything to avoid it. However, you are moderately interested in shared decision making because you think it would be best for the department, especially since most other departments function in this way.

You wonder what will happen in the upcoming department meeting.

Do not show this role sheet to anyone.

DEPARTMENTAL DILEMMA ROLE SHEET 5

Pat

You have been a researcher at Medway for three years. You are very vocal with the other researchers, to whom you have expressed confusion and annoyance with regard to Randall's actions; however, you say virtually nothing at department meetings and can be completely overpowered by Randall. The other researchers like you very much and are rather protective of you because they see you as vulnerable; they also are concerned about how you may be affected if issues become "hot" in the department because you cannot function under any pressure whatsoever.

In spite of the fact that you are easily intimidated professionally, you do an excellent job. Shared decision making interests you; you have confessed a lack of skills in this area, but you are willing to learn these skills and to try. You are glad that Elizabeth requested the upcoming meeting.

Do not show this role sheet to anyone.

DEPARTMENTAL DILEMMA ROLE SHEET 6

Dale

You are a good worker and you have good ideas. Although you are quite vocal in department meetings and will support others if you agree with them, at times you are unsure of yourself; therefore, you are not as strong in your stand on various issues as you might be. You are well liked, concerned about others, and interested in shared decision making.

You are annoyed by Randall's inability to deal with people better, and you hope that the upcoming meeting will be a first step toward improving relations between Randall and the other department members.

Do not show this role sheet to anyone.

DEPARTMENTAL DILEMMA ROLE SHEET 7

Kelly

You have been a researcher at Medway for only two years. You are outgoing and well liked by everyone. In addition, you are fair minded, enthusiastic about sharing the work load, and interested in shared decision making. Although you have good ideas and want to express them and to stand up for yourself during department meetings, you feel that Randall would find this behavior unacceptable. In the course of one department meeting, you brought up a policy suggestion to which Randall objected, and later he told you in private that "controversial issues" should be channeled through him before being raised in department meetings.

You plan to be cautious during the upcoming meeting unless someone else confronts Randall about his contradictory policies. If such confrontation occurs, you will speak up on the subject.

Do not show this role sheet to anyone.

DEPARTMENTAL DILEMMA ROLE SHEET 8

Terry

You are a new, inexperienced researcher. You are friendly and pleasant, but silent; you have revealed no interests, strengths, or viewpoints with regard to any of the issues raised in your presence. You plan to keep quiet but pay close attention during the upcoming meeting.

Do not show this role sheet to anyone.

351. TEAM PLANNING: EFFECTS OF DIFFERENTIAL INFORMATION

Goals

   I. To explore the dynamics of team planning.

   II. To examine the differences in communication, planning, and collaborative behavior when teams are given different amounts of information as the basis for completing a task.

Group Size

   Five teams of four to eight participants each.

Time Required

   Approximately two hours.

Materials

   I. One set of art supplies for each team. These supplies should include such items as paper, construction paper, straws, pipe cleaners, scissors, tape, and felt-tipped markers. Each team's set of supplies must not be visible until the appropriate time (see Process, Steps V and VI).

   II. A large tray for each team.

   III. One set of the appropriate instructions for each team. Each set is to be cut apart and the individual instructions distributed one at a time.

   IV. One copy of the Team Planning Observer Sheet for each observer.

   V. A pencil for each observer.

   VI. A clipboard or other portable writing surface for each observer.

Physical Setting

   A room with a large table on which the teams can display their models. In addition, each team should be provided with a table either in a separate room or in the same room. If only one room is available, the facilitator should plan carefully to ensure that each team can receive instructions, work, and construct its model in privacy.

Process

I. The participants are assembled into five groups that are designated Team A, Team B, Team C, Team D, and Team E.

II. The facilitator explains that the teams will be involved in a team-planning activity and that afterward they will be responsible for providing feedback regarding the process.

III. A volunteer is selected from each team to serve as an observer and is given a copy of the Team Planning Observer Sheet, a pencil, and a clipboard or other portable writing surface. Each observer is told that later he or she will report on the observations made during the experience.

IV. The teams are then asked to go to separate rooms or areas to await further instructions.

V. The facilitator gives each team its *first* instructions. In addition, Team E receives a set of art supplies and a tray. In answer to all questions, the facilitator replies, "You have been given all the information you require at this point."

VI. After fifteen minutes each team is provided with its *second* instructions. Teams A, B, C, and D are also provided with sets of art supplies and trays.

VII. After twenty minutes the facilitator gives each team its *third* instructions.

VIII. After fifteen minutes all teams are requested to bring their models to the main assembly area and to place them on the table.

IX. Each team is asked to meet separately to receive feedback from its observer regarding the procedures that were just completed. (Ten minutes.)

X. The facilitator briefly explains the instructions given to each team. Then each spokesperson is asked to explain his or her team's model to the total group and to clarify the ways in which the instructions affected both the team's organization and the final product. In addition, the team observers are asked to report briefly on their observations. (Thirty minutes.)

XI. The facilitator then leads a discussion of the entire activity, focusing on such concerns as the following:

1. The effects of the task instructions on the process and the finished product;

2. The effects of missing, partial, and complete instructions on the team decision-making, planning, and implementation periods; and

3. The extent to which each team is committed to its model and the implications of this commitment.

Variations

I. The activity may be introduced in Step II as one involving competition or collaboration. In this case appropriate criteria or selection methods should be introduced (consensus seeking, ranking, and so forth).

II. With a small group, one or more of Teams B, C, and D may be eliminated.

III. More specific instructions may be given to Teams D and E. For example, the instructions may include a list of factors that affect team communication or a picture of a model.

Similar Structured Experiences: *72 Annual:* Structured Experience **78, 82**; *Vol. V:* **163**; *'77 Annual:* **194**; *'78 Annual:* **221, 228**.

Suggested Instrument: *'77 Annual:* "TORI Group Self-Diagnosis Scale."

Notes on the Use of "Team Planning":

Submitted by Thomas J. Mallinson, Ron Sept, and Alan Tolliday.

TEAM PLANNING INSTRUCTIONS FOR TEAM A

Team A

Instruction 1: Spend fifteen minutes discussing the pros and cons of marriage.

Team A

Instruction 2: Using the set of art supplies that has been provided, work together to construct a model of team communication. You have twenty minutes to complete this task. If you complete the task before time is called, you may review your model, but you may not discuss the experience. Construct your model on the tray so that you can bring it with you later to display in the main assembly area.

Team A

Instruction 3: Spend fifteen minutes discussing this activity and selecting a spokesperson who will describe your model to the total group and explain how the instructions affected the team's organization and the final product.

TEAM PLANNING INSTRUCTIONS FOR TEAM B

Team B

Instruction 1: Spend fifteen minutes discussing the concepts or ideas that you believe are sufficiently important to be represented in any model of team communication.

Team B

Instruction 2: Using the set of art supplies that has been provided, work together to illustrate the points you have just discussed by constructing a model of team communication. You have twenty minutes to complete this task. If you complete the task before time is called, you may review your model, but you may not discuss the experience. Construct your model on the tray so that you can bring it with you later to display in the main assembly area.

Team B

Instruction 3: Spend fifteen minutes discussing this activity and selecting a spokesperson who will describe your model to the total group and explain how the instructions affected the team's organization and the final product.

TEAM PLANNING INSTRUCTIONS FOR TEAM C

Team C

Instruction 1: In fifteen minutes you will be required to carry out a task involving planning and construction. While you are waiting for the specific directions, discuss the resources of your team and the most effective way in which you can organize your resources to complete the task.

Team C

Instruction 2: Using the set of art supplies that has been provided, work together to construct a model of team communication. You have twenty minutes to complete this task. If you complete the task before time is called, you may review your model, but you may not discuss the experience. Construct your model on the tray so that you can bring it with you later to display in the main assembly area.

Team C

Instruction 3: Spend fifteen minutes discussing this activity and selecting a spokesperson who will describe your model to the total group and explain how the instructions affected the team's organization and the final product.

TEAM PLANNING INSTRUCTIONS FOR TEAM D

Team D

Instruction 1: In fifteen minutes you will be required to work together to construct a three-dimensional model of team communication by using art supplies that will be provided. Spend this preliminary period deciding which concepts or ideas you would like to see represented in your model and determining the most effective way in which to organize your resources for the task.

Team D

Instruction 2: Using your set of art supplies, work together to illustrate the points you have just discussed by constructing a model of team communication. You have twenty minutes to complete this task. If you complete the task before time is called, you may review your model, but you may not discuss the experience. Construct your model on the tray so that you can bring it with you later to display in the main assembly area.

Team D

Instruction 3: Spend fifteen minutes discussing this activity and selecting a spokesperson who will describe your model to the total group and explain how the instructions affected the team's organization and the final product.

TEAM PLANNING INSTRUCTIONS FOR TEAM E

Team E

Instruction 1: In fifteen minutes you will be required to work together to construct a three-dimensional model of team communication by using the set of art supplies that has been provided. Do not begin construction now; instead, use this preliminary period to decide which concepts and ideas you would like to see represented in your model and to determine the most effective way in which to organize your resources for the task.

Team E

Instruction 2: Using your set of art supplies, work together to illustrate the points you have just discussed by constructing a model of team communication. You have twenty minutes to complete this task. If you complete the task before time is called, you may review your model, but you may not discuss the experience. Construct your model on the tray so that you can bring it with you later to display in the main assembly area.

Team E

Instruction 3: Spend fifteen minutes discussing this activity and selecting a spokesperson who will describe your model to the total group and explain how the instructions affected the team's organization and the final product.

TEAM PLANNING OBSERVER SHEET

You are to observe a situation in which the members of a team complete the following three procedures:

1. Discussing an assigned topic (fifteen minutes);
2. Working together to construct a model of team communication (twenty minutes); and
3. Discussing the activity and selecting a spokesperson to describe their model to the total group and to explain how their instructions affected the team's organization and the final product (fifteen minutes).

Do not discuss this process, your instructions, or any aspect of the experience until you are instructed to do so. You are to make observations as described below. Space has been provided on this sheet so that you can make notes on your observations.

Instruction 1 (Procedure 1)

Watch the general pattern of *communication,* noting:

- The balance of participation and leadership roles:

- The ways in which the team members react to their instructions:

Instruction 2 (Procedure 2)

Watch the general pattern of *interaction,* noting:

- The ways in which the previous discussion influences the interaction process and the construction of the model:

- The extent to which member roles (for example, leadership) change from the first procedure to the second:

Instruction 3 (Procedure 3)

Watch the general pattern of *decision making*, noting:

- The criteria that the members use to select their spokesperson:

- The extent to which the members reach agreement regarding the final model and its rationale:

- Any changes in the model as a result of the discussion:

352. THE COMPANY TASK FORCE: DEALING WITH DISRUPTIVE BEHAVIOR

Goals

I. To help the participants to become aware of the roles and behaviors that are disruptive in meetings, the degree to which they are disruptive, and the positive as well as negative consequences associated with each.

II. To offer the participants an opportunity to develop strategies for dealing with disruptive roles and behaviors.

Group Size

Any number of groups of seven to nine participants each.

Time Required

Two and one-half hours.

Materials

I. A copy of The Company Task Force Background Sheet for each participant.

II. One set of The Company Task Force Role Sheets 1 through 9 for each group. Each group member is to receive a different sheet; Sheet 8 and/or Sheet 9 may be eliminated for any group consisting of fewer than nine members. (The facilitator may also want to have an extra copy of each role sheet available for distribution during Step XIII.)

III. Blank paper and a pencil for each group leader.

IV. A clipboard or other portable writing surface for each group leader.

Physical Setting

A room large enough so that each group can be seated in a circle and can work without disturbing the other groups. In addition, a separate room should be provided for the use of those group members who are designated as most obstructive.

Process

I. The facilitator tells the participants that they are to be involved in a role play and explains the goals of the activity.

II. Groups of seven to nine participants each are formed, and the members of each group are asked to be seated in a circle.

III. Copies of The Company Task Force Background Sheet are distributed, and the participants are asked to read this handout.

IV. A set of role sheets is distributed to each group in such a way that each member receives a different sheet. All participants are asked to read their sheets and are advised that they must maintain their roles during the role play.

V. The facilitator requests that the group leaders start their meetings.

VI. After fifteen minutes the facilitator stops the meetings and instructs all groups to remain intact. The members of each group are asked to spend ten minutes determining which role was the most obstructive.

VII. Each participant who is designated most obstructive by his or her group is asked to join the others so designated, to form a separate group in another room, and to await instructions.

VIII. The remaining participants are told that when the role play resumes, they are to assume new roles as cooperative, insightful people who are seriously working on the task-force problem. The facilitator then instructs each group to spend fifteen minutes establishing two strategies for dealing with its most obstructive member when that person returns; one strategy is to serve as the primary plan, and the other is to be used only if the first is unsuccessful.

IX. While the majority of the participants are working on their strategies, the facilitator asks the participants who were designated most obstructive to reflect on the positive aspects of their behaviors within their groups. (For example, The Rambler relieves tension, and The Organization Man/Woman provides valuable reminders of various obstacles to be overcome.) It is explained that when they return in approximately ten minutes, their groups will use specific strategies to deal with them. They are told to be sensitive to these strategies: If they are approached with humane attitudes, they are to respond in kind and adjust their behaviors to be more reasonable; however, if they are approached with aggression or in a demeaning way, they are to be creative in responding negatively and in character so that their groups can learn from their reactions. Finally, the obstructive members are asked to discuss ways to manifest their behaviors quickly when they return so that their groups can use the chosen strategies as soon as possible.

X. After the allotted time has passed, the obstructive members are asked to return to the main assembly room and to rejoin their groups. Then the facilitator instructs the groups to resume their meetings.

XI. After fifteen minutes the facilitator asks the groups to stop their role plays. Each group is instructed to discuss the experience; the nonobstructive members are asked to concentrate on whether the primary or backup strategy worked and how well, and the obstructive member is asked to concentrate on his or her reactions to the strategy(ies). Blank paper, pencils, and clipboards or other portable writing surfaces are distributed to the individual group leaders, who are asked to take notes during the discussions so that reports can be presented to the total group. (Fifteen minutes.)

XII. The total group is reconvened, and the facilitator asks the group leaders to take turns sharing the results of the discussions. (Ten minutes.)

XIII. The individual groups are reassembled. Each group is assigned one or two roles and is asked to determine the following for each role:

1. Positive features;

2. Negative features;

3. Interventions that might be used when dealing with this type of behavior in meetings; and

4. Ways in which these interventions might or might not be helpful.

(Twenty minutes.)

XIV. The total group is reconvened for a discussion of the results of the previous step and for summarizing. The following question is useful in concluding the experience: If you were to give advice on handling disruptive people, what would it be?

Variations

I. The activity may be shortened by eliminating Step XIII.

II. After Step XII copies of the lecturette entitled "Dealing with Disruptive Individuals in Meetings" (from "Lecturette Sources") may be distributed and the groups' strategies compared with those presented in the lecturette.

III. In Step XIV each participant may be asked to select a partner, to discuss with the partner a disruptive person with whom he or she must interact, and to develop a strategy for dealing with this person.

IV. The role play may be run in a group-on-group configuration, with the majority of participants observing as one group conducts its meeting. Subsequently, the observers report on the factors listed in Step XIII.

Similar Structured Experiences: *Vol. I:* Structured Experience **9**; *'75 Annual:* **139**; *'77 Annual:* **192**; *'81 Annual:* **290**.

Suggested Instrument: *'81 Annual:* "The Group Incidents Questionnaire (GIQ): A Measure of Skill in Group Facilitation."

Lecturette Sources: *'74 Annual:* "Hidden Agendas"; *'79 Annual:* "Encouraging Others to Change Their Behavior"; *'80 Annual:* "Dealing with Disruptive Individuals in Meetings"; *'83 Annual:* "Stress, Communication, and Assertiveness: A Framework for Interpersonal Problem Solving."

Notes on the Use of "The Company Task Force":

Submitted by Susanne W. Whitcomb.

THE COMPANY TASK FORCE BACKGROUND SHEET

You are an employee of Organic Foodstuffs, Inc., a company that has been manufacturing vitamins and food supplements in the town of Belmont Shore since 1913. Gradually the residential areas of the town have encircled the company's factory, and complaints from those who live nearby have been escalating over the last few years. These complaints generally involve air and water pollution, residential-parking abuses, the piercing sound of the 8:00 a.m. whistle, and lunch-time littering. The company president has recently joined the Community Service League, and since then he has become aware of the extent of the factory's unpopularity. Consequently, he has appointed a task force of employees to address the company's poor image. You are a member of this task force, which is meeting today to determine recommendations to be submitted to the president immediately afterward.

THE COMPANY TASK FORCE ROLE SHEET 1

The Leader

You have been appointed by the company president to be the leader of the task force. As the leader, your basic responsibilities are to accomplish the following:

- Keep the discussion flowing and on track;
- Control the members who try to dominate the discussion; and
- Ensure that the session results in specific recommendations of ways to improve the company's image.

At the beginning of the meeting, you introduce yourself as the officially appointed leader, emphasize the seriousness of the task at hand, and elicit ideas for image improvement.

Do not show this role description to anyone.

THE COMPANY TASK FORCE ROLE SHEET 2

The Power Monger

You want to usurp the leadership role from the officially appointed leader and make a big impression on the other task-force members. You have no real interest in the task at hand; instead, your objective is to obtain some of the power you need in order to bring to fruition your "pet" project: convincing the company to open a branch office in Tahiti. Once you have assumed control of the task force, your plan is to switch the focus of the meeting to your project. At this point you hope to gain support for the project by emphasizing its positive points. For example, opening the branch office will:

- Attract worldwide publicity;
- Show the company's concern for world affairs; and
- Bring fame to Belmont Shore.

Do not show this role description to anyone.

Structured Experience 352

THE COMPANY TASK FORCE ROLE SHEET 3

The Pain in the Neck

You are the negative member of the task force. The other members appear to be extremely poorly organized, and you fail to see how anything can be accomplished in this meeting. In fact, you do not understand why you were appointed to the task force; you have nothing to contribute, and you resent the fact that you have to take time from your busy work schedule to attend. You are hoping to convince the others that the task is impossible and should be abandoned.

Do not show this role description to anyone.

THE COMPANY TASK FORCE ROLE SHEET 4

The Idealist

You have a deep, spiritual commitment to eliminating pollution. You feel that the entire focus of the task force is wrong; the appropriate task is not to reverse the company's negative image, but to put an end to the abuses for which the complaints have been received. It is important to you that the company be concerned not only with its own welfare, but also with that of the entire world.

Because you cannot compromise your values by helping to complete the assigned task, you try to persuade the other members to adopt your viewpoint and work on solving the real problem.

Do not show this role description to anyone.

THE COMPANY TASK FORCE ROLE SHEET 5

The Rambler

In this meeting, as in all others that you attend, you cannot stay focused on the subject at hand. You have an active but undisciplined mind, and the comments made at meetings frequently remind you of unrelated anecdotes and bits of news or information that your gregarious nature compels you to share aloud.

Do not show this role description to anyone.

THE COMPANY TASK FORCE ROLE SHEET 6

The Organization Man/Woman

You are highly conscious of the formal organizational hierarchy; during your career with the company you have always been careful to proceed through the "right channels," obey the rules, and adhere to the established norms. Your instinct for professional survival makes you extremely cautious; in fact, you refuse to act on any idea until you are certain that it meets the company standards. Consequently, you maintain a wary stance throughout this meeting. You feel responsible for reminding the others that trying to change the company's regular operating procedures may be dangerous and that those in authority must make the ultimate decisions.

Do not show this role description to anyone.

THE COMPANY TASK FORCE ROLE SHEET 7

The Mediator

You cannot stand conflict and you believe that compromise is always possible. Consequently, during the meeting you make a concerted effort to maintain harmony among the members of the task force. You feel compelled to remind the others when appropriate that all viewpoints are worth hearing, that most positions on issues are not all that different, and that everyone should have a chance to participate in the process of establishing recommendations.

Do not show this role description to anyone.

THE COMPANY TASK FORCE ROLE SHEET 8

The Veteran

You have been employed with the company twice as long as any other member of the task force. In your opinion the current situation with the company's image does not warrant operational changes. During your long period of employment, you have seen a number of practices implemented and then abandoned; you believe that changes arising from the image problem will fall into the same category. In addition, over the years you have learned why certain approaches have failed and why they will continue to fail in the future. Consequently, you feel it is important to let the others know when they suggest alternatives that have proven ineffective in the past.

Do not show this role description to anyone.

THE COMPANY TASK FORCE ROLE SHEET 9

The Silent One

Attending meetings is always difficult for you because you are too shy and reserved to participate actively. You are professionally insecure and believe that your opinion, even when elicited, is not worth stating. When the others ask for your input, you are forced to tell them that although you find the discussion interesting, you are present only to listen and to learn.

Do not show this role description to anyone.

353. MANAGEMENT SKILLS: ASSESSING PERSONAL PERFORMANCE

Goals

I. To heighten the participants' awareness of the wide range of behaviors that are encompassed by management.

II. To enable the participants to assess their own needs for changes in their management-related behaviors.

Group Size

Any number of triads.

Time Required

One hour and twenty-five minutes.

Materials

I. A copy of the Management Skills Inventory for each participant.

II. A pencil for each participant.

III. A clipboard or other portable writing surface for each participant.

Physical Setting

A room with movable chairs for the participants.

Process

I. The facilitator distributes copies of the Management Skills Inventory and pencils and asks each participant to complete this instrument. (Twenty minutes.)

II. The participants are assembled into triads. The members of each triad are instructed to help one another to develop ways to improve in areas of deficiency as well as ways to gauge and monitor improvement. (Thirty minutes.)

III. The total group is reassembled to discuss the experience. The following questions are helpful:

1. What did this instrument tell you about your management skills? How do you feel about the way you assessed yourself?
2. Were you previously aware that you used the types of behavior dealt with in the instrument?
3. Did the items in the instrument differ from the behaviors that you feel are necessary for managers? If so, how? Are there any that you do not feel are necessary? Are there any necessary ones that were not included in the instrument?
4. Did you uncover any areas of activity that you have neglected? any biases that may require examination?
5. With regard to any of the behaviors dealt with in the instrument, do you conduct yourself in a particular way because of established norms within your organization? Would you change your behavior if these norms did not exist? Why or why not?
6. What types of activities are you prepared to begin to work on?

Variations

I. Staff members may be asked to predict one another's responses to particular items and subsequently to compare their predictions with actual responses.

II. The participants may be asked to develop a set of organizational learning skills from the responses and the discussions.

III. The entire group may be reassembled several times over a long period to complete the instrument and to study improvement.

Similar Structured Experiences: *Vol. I:* Structured Experience 3; *Vol. VIII:* **296**; *Vol. IX:* **345**.

Suggested Instruments: *'72 Annual:* "Supervisory Attitudes: The X-Y Scale"; *'73 Annual:* "LEAD (Leadership: Employee Orientation and Differentiation) Questionnaire"; *76 Annual:* "Leader Effectiveness and Adaptability Description (LEAD)"; *'81 Annual:* "Patterns of Effective Supervisory Behavior"; *'83 Annual:* "The TEM Survey."

Lecturette Sources: *'72 Annual:* "Criteria of Effective Goal-Setting: The SPIRO Model"; *74 Annual:* "The 'Shouldist' Manager"; *75 Annual:* "The Supervisor as Counselor"; *76 Annual:* "Leadership as Persuasion and Adaptation"; *'77 Annual:* "A Practical Leadership Paradigm"; *79 Annual:* "The Centered Boss."

Submitted by Carol J. Levin.

Notes on the Use of "Management Skills":

MANAGEMENT SKILLS INVENTORY

Instructions: This form is designed to stimulate your thinking about your skills and relationships with others as a manager. It is intended to help you to set your own goals for development. The steps for using it are as follows:

1. Read through the list of activities and decide for each one whether you are performing it to a sufficient extent or whether you need to do it to a greater or lesser extent. Mark an X for each item in the appropriate blank. Some activities that you feel are important may not be listed. Blank lines are provided in each category so that such an item may be added.

2. Go back over the entire list, choose the three or four items on which you would most like to improve at this time, and mark each of these items with an asterisk.

3. List the three or four activities in the space provided under "Action Plan." Then make preliminary notes about specific actions that you might take to improve your performance in each of these areas. Later you will be asked to share these notes with others who will help you to develop a final plan.

	Present Performance Sufficient	Need to Do More	Need to Do Less
Communicating Skills			
1. Making clear statements	——	——	——
2. Being brief and concise	——	——	——
3. Being forceful	——	——	——
4. Drawing others out	——	——	——
5. Listening alertly	——	——	——
6. Checking out assumptions	——	——	——
7. Writing clearly and effectively	——	——	——
8. _____	——	——	——

Adapted from "Goals for Personal Development Inventory," in J.W. Pfeiffer and J.E. Jones (Eds.), *The 1976 Annual Handbook for Group Facilitators*, p. 59, University Associates, 1976.

	Present Performance Sufficient	Need to Do More	Need to Do Less
Problem-Solving/Decision-Making Skills			
9. Defining problem or goal	———	———	———
10. Establishing criteria for solutions	———	———	———
11. Asking for and researching alternative ideas and opinions	———	———	———
12. Giving ideas and opinions	———	———	———
13. Evaluating ideas critically before choosing one	———	———	———
14. Evaluating results of the solution or decision	———	———	———
15. _____	———	———	———
Planning Skills			
16. Establishing a clear goal or mission statement	———	———	———
17. Determining specific objectives	———	———	———
18. Involving others in the planning process	———	———	———
19. Foreseeing barriers	———	———	———
20. Developing contingency plans	———	———	———
21. Integrating budget into the planning process	———	———	———
22. Evaluating results on a regular basis	———	———	———
23. _____	———	———	———
Staffing Skills			
24. Developing clear job descriptions	———	———	———
25. Recruiting appropriate candidates.	———	———	———

	Present Performance Sufficient	Need to Do More	Need to Do Less
26. Interviewing fairly and effectively	___	___	___
27. Negotiating salary and/or benefits fairly and effectively	___	___	___
28. Evaluating performance on a regular basis	___	___	___
29. Terminating when appropriate	___	___	___
30. Providing ongoing supervision (coaching and feedback on a frequent basis)	___	___	___
31. _____	___	___	___

Organizing Skills

	Present Performance Sufficient	Need to Do More	Need to Do Less
32. Clarifying work flow	___	___	___
33. Establishing departments or units as needed	___	___	___
34. Developing coordination between units	___	___	___
35. Holding effective meetings as necessary	___	___	___
36. Delegating tasks to others	___	___	___
37. Developing systems to improve or simplify task accomplishment	___	___	___
38. _____	___	___	___

Group-Dynamics Skills

	Present Performance Sufficient	Need to Do More	Need to Do Less
39. Initiating ideas	___	___	___
40. Clarifying and elaborating on discussion	___	___	___

	Present Performance Sufficient	Need to Do More	Need to Do Less
41. Summarizing others' ideas	——	——	——
42. Gatekeeping (ensuring that people are heard)	——	——	——
43. Compromising or mediating	——	——	——
44. Standard testing	——	——	——
45. Consensus seeking	——	——	——
46. Noting tension and interest levels in a group	——	——	——
47. Encouraging	——	——	——
48. Noting when the group avoids a topic	——	——	——
49. Sensing individuals' feelings	——	——	——
50. Recognizing and understanding the stages of group development	——	——	——
51. Controlling dysfunctional behavior	——	——	——
52. _____	——	——	——

Morale-Building Skills

53. Showing interest in individuals	——	——	——
54. Expressing praise or appreciation	——	——	——
55. Consulting with employees before making decisions that affect them	——	——	——
56. Providing opportunities for growth and development	——	——	——
57. Promoting from within	——	——	——
58. Treating people fairly and equitably	——	——	——
59. Helping people to reach agreement; harmonizing	——	——	——

	Present Performance Sufficient	Need to Do More	Need to Do Less
60. Upholding rights of individuals in the face of group pressure	_____	_____	_____
61. _____	_____	_____	_____

General/Personal Skills

62. Telling personal feelings to others	_____	_____	_____
63. Facing and accepting conflict and anger	_____	_____	_____
64. Facing and accepting closeness and affection	_____	_____	_____
65. Understanding personal motivation (self-insight)	_____	_____	_____
66. Soliciting feedback on personal behavior	_____	_____	_____
67. Accepting help willingly	_____	_____	_____
68. Criticizing self constructively	_____	_____	_____
69. Managing stress and tension	_____	_____	_____
70. Managing time effectively (setting priorities)	_____	_____	_____
71. Taking good care of self (nutrition, rest, etc.)	_____	_____	_____
72. Taking time for relaxation and recreation	_____	_____	_____
73. _____	_____	_____	_____

Action Plan

Activity	Actions to Take to Improve Performance

1.

2.

3.

4.

354. THE MANAGER'S GUIDEBOOK: UNDERSTANDING MOTIVATION

Goals

I. To provide the participants with a situation in which the issues of motivation can be explored.

II. To help the participants to enhance their understanding of the concept of motivation.

Group Size

Five groups of four to seven participants each.

Time Required

Approximately two and one-half hours.

Materials

I. A copy of The Manager's Guidebook Instruction Sheet for each participant.

II. A copy of The Manager's Guidebook Discussion Sheet for each participant.

III. An assortment of art supplies to be used by the groups in creating guidebooks. These supplies should include items such as blank paper, construction paper, pencils, pens, felt-tipped markers, scissors, tape, and staplers.

IV. A newsprint flip chart and a felt-tipped marker or a chalkboard and chalk.

Physical Setting

A table and chairs for each group. An additional table should be provided for the purpose of displaying the assortment of art supplies.

Process

I. The facilitator explains the goals of the activity, forms five groups of four to seven participants each, distributes copies of The Manager's Guidebook Instruction Sheet, and instructs the participants to read the handout.

II. The members of each group are asked to decide who will assume the roles of manager, artist, presenter, and one or more assistants. Questions are elicited, and the task is clarified as necessary.

III. The facilitator instructs the managers to take whatever art supplies they wish from the display table, emphasizing that what is displayed is all that is available. Then the groups are told to begin. During the hour allotted for completion of the guidebooks, the facilitator monitors the activities of the various groups and keeps the participants informed about the amount of time remaining.

IV. After the hour has passed, all groups are asked to stop working on their guidebooks. Then the presenters are invited to take turns presenting guidebooks to the total group. The participants are instructed to listen carefully to these presentations; while listening they are to evaluate each guidebook according to the criteria listed on the instruction sheet. (Thirty minutes.)

V. The facilitator elicits comments regarding the strengths of each guidebook and lists these strengths on newsprint or a chalkboard. (Ten minutes.)

VI. The members of each group are given copies of The Manager's Guidebook Discussion Sheet and are asked to discuss answers to the questions on this handout. Each group is instructed to appoint a reporter to take notes during the discussion and report later to the total group. The facilitator ensures that the reporters have blank paper and pencils or pens to use in completing their task. (Twenty minutes.)

VII. The reporters share the findings of their groups, and the total group discusses what has been learned about motivation and ways in which the participants can apply their learnings to their personal and professional lives.

Variations

I. Competition may be fostered by stipulating at the outset that a vote will be taken to determine the best guidebook. In addition, a reward may be offered for the team that creates the winning guidebook.

II. The facilitator may privately instruct the managers to employ different leadership styles (autocratic, democratic, and so forth) and then elicit the group members' comments regarding the effects of these styles on their motivation to complete the task.

III. If one or more groups are unable to finish their guidebooks in an hour and if more time is available, the facilitator may ask the managers to leave their groups, discuss the situation among themselves, and arrive at a unanimous decision either to allow or to disallow additional time. Subsequently, during the final processing, the participants are asked to evaluate the functioning of their groups in the managers' absence.

IV. The facilitator may present a lecturette on motivation at the end of Step V.

Similar Structured Experiences: *'73 Annual:* Structured Experience **100**; *Vol. VI:* **204**; *'79 Annual:* **244**; *Vol. VII:* **253**.

Suggested Instrument: *'73 Annual:* "Motivation Feedback Opinionnaire."

Lecturette Sources: *'72 Annual:* "The Maslow Need Hierarchy"; *'83 Annual:* "Encouragement: Giving Positive Invitations."

Notes on the Use of "The Manager's Guidebook":

Submitted by Kenneth L. Murrell.

THE MANAGER'S GUIDEBOOK INSTRUCTION SHEET

The task assigned to your group is to use the art supplies that will be provided to create a *manager's guidebook to motivating*. The members of your group will assume different roles while working on this task: manager, artist, presenter, and one or more assistants. The *manager* will serve as the group leader or supervisor; the *artist* will execute the final product; the *presenter* will describe your guidebook to the total group; and the *assistant(s)* will provide whatever help you deem necessary and appropriate.

You may construct the guidebook in any way you wish; its content, format, and design are strictly up to you, as is the specific interpretation of the roles described above. However, you should keep in mind that each guidebook should meet the following criteria:

- Usefulness of content;
- Clarity and understandability of concepts;
- Attractiveness of appearance; and
- Effectiveness of presentation to the total group.

You have one hour in which to complete this task.

THE MANAGER'S GUIDEBOOK DISCUSSION SHEET

1. Did your manager collect adequate art supplies to create the guidebook? If not, how did you feel about working with insufficient resources? Did this situation affect your attitude toward completing the project?

2. What approach did your manager take in supervising the project? What was the effect of this approach on your motivation?

3. How well did the members of your group work together? How well did they communicate with each other? Did the communication process affect your level of motivation? If so, in what way?

4. Did some members work harder than others? If so, why?

5. How did motivation levels differ among the members of your group? How motivated were the manager, the artist, the presenter, and the assistant(s) and why?

6. What was your major concern in completing the task?

7. If you were asked to begin a similar activity at this point, how motivated would you feel? In view of your present feelings, what factors seem to affect your personal level of motivation?

8. If you were to evaluate your group according to the concepts presented in your guidebook, how would it fare?

355. FEEDBACK: INCREASING SELF-PERCEPTIONS

Goals

    I. To facilitate the process of giving and receiving feedback in a group.

    II. To help the participants to understand the feedback that they receive.

    III. To promote a process for exploring the participants' "hidden" characteristics.

Group Size

All members of an intact group. (If the group consists of more than six members, the activity may be conducted in subgroups or in more than one session.)

Time Required

Approximately two hours.

Materials

    I. For each participant, enough 3" x 5" index cards to equal the number of other participants. (For example, if there are five participants, each participant receives four 3" x 5" cards.)

    II. A pencil for each participant.

    III. A sheet of newsprint and a felt-tipped marker for each participant.

    IV. Masking tape.

Physical Setting

A room with chairs and writing surfaces for the participants.

Process

    I. The facilitator presents a lecturette on·"The Johari Window"[1] and the process of giving and receiving feedback. (Fifteen minutes.)

---

[1]See P.C. Hanson, "The Johari Window: A Model for Soliciting and Giving Feedback," in J.E. Jones & J.W. Pfeiffer (Eds.), *The 1973 Annual Handbook for Group Facilitators*, University Associates, 1973.

II. The facilitator announces that the members are to participate in a process whereby they provide one another with feedback for the purpose of increasing each member's self-knowledge. Each participant is given 3″ x 5″ index cards and a pencil. Then the facilitator gives the following instructions:

"Take one of the cards and write 'From ＿＿(blank)＿＿ to ＿＿(blank)＿＿,' inserting your name and that of any other member, respectively, in the blanks; underneath this line write three adjectives or short phrases that describe your own perception of the other member's 'hidden' characteristics. Try to be specific so that the member being described will receive useful feedback. After you have completed this task, do the same for every other member of the group."

(Fifteen minutes.)

III. The participants are asked to distribute their cards to the appropriate members.

IV. The facilitator distributes sheets of newsprint and felt-tipped markers and instructs each participant to write his or her name at the top of the sheet and then to list all feedback items provided by every fellow member. It is explained that the sources of the various items need not be identified. (Ten minutes.)

V. Each participant is asked to review his or her list, identifying and underlining items of particular concern or interest. (Five minutes.)

VI. The participants are provided with masking tape and are instructed to post their lists and to spend a few minutes reviewing all posted data.

VII. The facilitator reconvenes the group for a discussion period during which each participant is allowed a maximum of ten minutes to review his or her list with the fellow members. It is emphasized that this process should consist of requesting clarification and assessing how widely shared some of the opinions may be; justification and argument are not permissible.

VIII. After the discussion has been concluded, the facilitator invites the participants to share their reactions to the experience. The following questions may be helpful:

1. How did you feel about the balance between positive and negative adjectives used to describe you?

2. How do these adjectives compare with your perception of yourself? What did you learn about the ways in which others perceive you? How do you feel about what you learned? Are there any other thoughts that you would like to express?

3. Based on this experience, what would you like to change about yourself? How could you go about changing? How could the other members of the group help you with the change process?

Variations

I. At a subsequent meeting of the group, the participants may be invited to explore further certain personal characteristics that previously may have been hidden from others. The facilitator explains that for an hour the participants may discuss these characteristics and that the following rules will apply:

1. Anyone may ask a fellow member any question.
2. The member being questioned has the right to decline answering by saying, "I pass on that question."
3. If the questioned member decides to answer, he or she agrees to do so as fully as possible.

II. The group may choose to concentrate on either positive or negative adjectives.

III. The feedback may be given in forms other than adjectives that describe the person in question. For example, experiential statements such as the following may be completed: "When I am with you, I feel. . . ."

Similar Structured Experiences: *Vol. I:* Structured Experiences **13, 17**; *Vol. III:* **58**; *'73 Annual:* **97, 99**; *Vol. IV:* **107**; *Vol. V:* **168, 170**; *'78 Annual:* **225**; *Vol. VIII:* **315**; *'82 Annual:* **326**.

Suggested Instruments: *Vol. III:* "Feedback Rating Scales"; *77 Annual:* "Interpersonal Check List (ICL)."

Lecturette Sources: *'73 Annual:* "The Johari Window: A Model for Soliciting and Giving Feedback"; *76 Annual:* "Interpersonal Feedback as Consensual Validation of Constructs," "Making Judgments Descriptive."

Notes on the Use of "Feedback":

Submitted by Cyril R. Mill.

356. MESSAGES: A GROUP FEEDBACK EXPERIENCE

Goals

I. To examine the thought process, verbal behavior, and risk factor involved in sending verbal messages about feelings.

II. To analyze the ways in which the process of sending and receiving such messages contributes to group cohesiveness.

Group Size

Four to twenty participants who have worked together in a common group experience.

Time Required

Approximately forty-five minutes.

Materials

I. A sheet of paper and a pen or a felt-tipped marker for each participant.

II. A copy of the Messages Instruction Sheet for each participant.

Physical Setting

A chair and a writing surface for each participant. The chairs should be arranged so that each participant can see all of the others.

Process

I. The facilitator introduces the activity:

"When we attempt to express our feelings verbally, the spontaneity and empathy of these feelings are often distorted by the thinking process itself. It is not uncommon to hear ourselves express feelings in statements such as 'I *think* I'd like to say...' or 'I *thought* I'd like to tell you....' In essence, the problem with expressing feelings verbally is that we 'filter' our messages through the thinking mode. Before speaking, the person sending a message usually analyzes three factors:

- The potential value of the message to the recipient;

- Whether the message will be acknowledged with approval or disapproval; and
- The degree of likelihood that the message will expose the recipient to embarrassment and/or the sender to humiliation.

However, there are times when each of us would like to be able to communicate feelings verbally without engaging in the filtering process; sometimes it is not only appropriate but also desirable to express feelings openly and honestly, without reluctance and without prior evaluation of the benefits and consequences involved. The activity that you are about to experience is intended to help you to do this."

II. Each participant is given a sheet of paper, a pen or a felt-tipped marker, and a copy of the Messages Instruction Sheet. Everyone is asked to read the instructions and to begin. (Ten minutes.)

III. After all participants have completed the task, they are asked to take turns presenting their cards to the group by reading aloud the messages written on these cards. It is specified that no verbal feedback is to be given during this step.

IV. In response to the messages read during the previous step, the participants are invited to give any feedback or to make any statements they wish.

V. The facilitator states that although we often send actual greeting cards to others on special occasions, we seldom realize how important it is to send verbal "greeting cards" to develop interpersonal trust and cohesiveness within a group. It is also mentioned that during a group experience, it is important for the members to express their feelings about that experience in an open and honest manner. Then the facilitator leads a discussion of the entire activity by asking the following questions:

1. How successful were you in avoiding the filtering process? How did you try to avoid it?

2. What were your feelings and/or fears as you read your message? after you read it? How did you assess the impact of your message without verbal feedback?

3. What is your experience of the level of trust in your group at this moment?

4. What do you require from others in order to express your feelings spontaneously?

5. What else would you like to express at this time?

Variations

I. The facilitator may make the greeting-card assignment specific to a particular stage of group development. For example, the participants may be asked to use a theme of announcement, friendship, or group closure.

II. In Step III the participants may be instructed to express their messages nonverbally.

III. Steps III and IV may be combined so that when the participants read their messages, they may elicit and/or receive verbal feedback at that time.

Similar Structured Experiences: *Vol. III:* Structured Experiences **56, 65**; *Vol. IV:* **104**; *'75 Annual:* **146**; *Vol. V:* **168**; *'77 Annual:* **190**; *'78 Annual:* **225**.

Suggested Instruments: *Vol. III:* "Group-Climate Inventory," "Group-Growth Evaluation Form," "Feedback Rating Scales," Postmeeting Reactions Form"; *'77 Annual:* "TORI Group Self-Diagnosis Scale"; *'81 Annual:* "Work-Group-Effectiveness Inventory."

Lecturette Sources: *'73 Annual:* "Risk-Taking," "Thinking and Feeling"; *'81 Annual:* "Thinking About Feelings."

Notes on the Use of "Messages":

Submitted by Gilles L. Talbot.

MESSAGES INSTRUCTION SHEET

Using the materials that you have been given, create a greeting card to be "sent" to this group. The message on your card should express the feelings you have experienced as a member of the group. You need not write your message in verse or rhyme unless you choose to do so. What is important is that the words you use convey your feelings openly, honestly, and without reluctance. Remember to avoid expressions such as "I think" that tend to dilute your feelings.

357. GROUP SELL: ADVERTISING GROUP VALUES

Goals

I. To explore the participants' reasons for joining groups and the attractiveness of different types of groups.

II. To examine issues concerning group loyalties and values about groups.

Group Size

A minimum of twenty and a maximum of fifty participants.

Time Required

One and one-half to two hours.

Materials

I. One set of Group Sell Leader Sheets 1 through 5 (a different sheet for each of five group leaders). If desired, extra copies of these sheets may be made available to the leaders to distribute to members of their groups.

II. One copy of the Group Sell Discussion Sheet for each participant.

III. Blank paper and a pencil for each participant.

IV. Newsprint and a felt-tipped marker for each leader.

V. Masking tape.

Physical Setting

A main assembly room in which the participants can move about freely. It is preferable, but not essential, to have five large tables (one for each group) in this room; if no tables are available, portable writing surfaces should be provided. A chair for each participant during the latter stages of the activity (Steps VII and VIII) is also optional.

A separate room with a table and chairs should be provided for the purpose of group-leader preparation.

Process

I. The facilitator introduces the activity as one that involves recruiting members for groups and then calls for five volunteers to serve as group leaders.

II. The facilitator announces that he or she and the group leaders will be leaving the room for fifteen minutes to prepare for the activity. The remaining participants are given blank paper and pencils and are asked to make lists of the groups to which they currently belong and then discuss these groups until the facilitator and the group leaders return.

III. In a separate room, each group leader is given a copy of a different leader sheet. The facilitator outlines the activity, explaining that the leaders will be "selling" their respective groups to the remaining participants. It is emphasized that the leaders must maintain their roles so that distinctions among the groups are ensured. Blank paper, pencils, newsprint, and felt-tipped markers are distributed. Then each leader is asked to spend the remainder of the fifteen minutes studying his or her sheet, determining an effective approach to member recruitment, making notes as desired, and creating a newsprint poster to advertise his or her group.

IV. After the allotted time has passed, the group leaders are asked to return to the main assembly room and to bring their notes and posters with them. The facilitator makes an announcement:

"Each of these five people is the leader of a different kind of group, and for the next *half-hour* all five will be soliciting your membership in their respective groups. The leaders and some or all of the new recruits they obtain will provide you with information about their groups and/or try to persuade you to join. You must decide to join *only one* group, but you may switch groups at any time until it is announced that the joining period is over. I will keep you apprised of the amount of time left in which to make your final decision."

V. Each group leader is stationed in a different location in the room and is given masking tape with which to attach his or her newsprint poster to the wall at this location. Then the participants are asked to begin.

VI. The facilitator monitors the activities throughout the room, announcing the remaining time at intervals until one-half hour has passed, at which point it is announced that the joining period is over.

VII. Each group is asked to remain intact at its station. The facilitator distributes copies of the Group Sell Discussion Sheet and requests that each group select a reporter to record answers to the questions on the discussion sheet and then report on these answers later. Each group is given blank paper and a pencil to be used by the reporter. (Twenty minutes.)

Structured Experience

VIII. The total group is reassembled. Each reporter is asked to share his or her group's data, and the facilitator leads a discussion of the data and summarizes the reactions.

Variations

I. This structured experience may be used with an ongoing group by assigning leader roles one session in advance of the activity itself.

II. With an ongoing group, the following questions may be added at the end of the discussion sheet:

1. Can you compare your *real* group with one or several of the imaginary groups created for this activity? What are the similarities and differences?

2. What kind of image do you think your *real* group projects?

3. What would you like potential members to think about your *real* group?

4. Can you apply what you have experienced here to improving your *real* group?

III. The facilitator may create an option for the participants not to join any group. In this case the discussion sheet should be altered accordingly, and a reporter should be chosen to represent those who decide to remain unaffiliated.

IV. The group leaders may be instructed to fashion their approaches so that their groups are not attractive. This task creates dissonance among the participants as they try to decide among the groups.

Similar Structured Experiences: *72 Annual:* Structured Experience **77**; *'74 Annual:* **129**; *'81 Annual:* **282**; *Vol. VIII:* **296**.

Suggested Instrument: *75 Annual:* "Diagnosing Organization Ideology."

Lecturette Sources: *72 Annual:* "Job Enrichment"; *'82 Annual:* "Issues Present When Entering a System."

Submitted by Tim A. Flanagan.

Notes on the Use of "Group Sell":

GROUP SELL LEADER SHEET 1

Bribery Group

Your group exists only because its members have been promised something in return for joining. Prospective members are offered whatever may appeal to them: money, all-expense-paid trips, success in life or business, and so forth. The group's goal is to have as many members as possible.

As the leader of this group, your objective is to solicit new members. You may use any tactic that is *consistent with the description of the group* provided in the preceding paragraph. Anyone who joins your group may assist you in recruiting others by reading this sheet and following these directions.

Do not show this sheet to nonmembers.

GROUP SELL LEADER SHEET 2

Elite Group

Your group is traditionally considered "high class" and perhaps even snobbish. High standards are emphasized. Prospective members are interviewed carefully; only those who "measure up" are invited to join.

As the leader of this group, your objective is to solicit new members. You may use any tactic that is *consistent with the description of the group* in the preceding paragraph. Anyone who joins your group may assist you in recruiting others by reading this sheet and following these directions.

Do not show this sheet to nonmembers.

GROUP SELL LEADER SHEET 3

Productive Group

Your group exists not only because of its accomplishments, but also by virtue of its goals: learning, working, and developing comradeship among members. Prospective members are given an accurate description of life within the group and then are encouraged to make their own decisions regarding joining.

As the leader of this group, your objective is to solicit new members. You may use any tactic that is *consistent with the description of the group* in the preceding paragraph. Anyone who joins your group may assist you in recruiting others by reading this sheet and following these directions.

Do not show this sheet to nonmembers.

GROUP SELL LEADER SHEET 4

Power Group

Your group has the authority to do and act as it pleases. It exerts influence, makes policies, and exercises control over the actions of nonmembers. Prospective members must be willing to use the power of the group.

As the leader of this group, your objective is to solicit new members. You may use any tactic that is *consistent with the description of the group* in the preceding paragraph. Anyone who joins your group may assist you in recruiting others by reading this sheet and following these directions.

Do not show this sheet to nonmembers.

GROUP SELL LEADER SHEET 5

Party Group

Your group's exclusive purpose is to have fun. Prospective members are told that their only responsibility, if they join the group, will be to enjoy themselves and to contribute to the enjoyment of the other members.

As the leader of this group, your objective is to solicit new members. You may use any tactic that is *consistent with the description of the group* in the preceding paragraph. Anyone who joins your group may assist you in recruiting others by reading this sheet and following these directions.

Do not show this sheet to nonmembers.

GROUP SELL DISCUSSION SHEET

1. What attracted you to your group?

2. How would you characterize the values of the different groups? How did you react to their different recruiting approaches?

3. As a recruited member of your group, what did you look for in potential members?

4. Did anyone switch groups? If so, what were the reasons? Would anyone like to switch groups now? What would induce you to do so?

5. How satisfied were you with your choice?

6. How loyal did you feel to your group? How would you explain the link between the values your group espouses and your loyalty to the group?

7. After joining your group, did you help to solicit members? Why or why not? If you did help to solicit, how did you do so? What does this say about your commitment to your group?

8. What do you look for in a group or organization that you are considering joining? How does this fit with the choices you made in this experience?

9. How do your current memberships in real groups fit with what you have learned during this activity?

358. INTERVIEWING: GATHERING PERTINENT INFORMATION

Goals

I. To help the participants to become familiar with the interviewing process from the interviewer's perspective.

II. To allow the participants to practice developing criteria that a job candidate must meet based on the nature and duties of the job.

III. To assist the participants in developing ways to elicit pertinent information from job candidates.

Group Size

Three to ten triads.

Time Required

One hour and forty-five minutes.

Materials

I. Blank paper and a pencil for each participant.

II. A newsprint flip chart and a felt-tipped marker or a chalkboard and chalk.

Physical Setting

Any room in which the triads can work without disturbing one another. Writing surfaces should be provided for the participants.

Process

I. The facilitator delivers a lecturette on the process of interviewing from the interviewer's perspective. It is emphasized that before any interviews take place, the interviewer must determine the following:

1. The exact nature and duties of the job in question;

2. The skills and characteristics that a person must have in order to succeed in the job; and

3. Ways to elicit pertinent information from job candidates.

(Ten minutes.)

II. The facilitator briefly explains the activity and its goals. The participants brainstorm a list of jobs while the facilitator records these jobs on newsprint or a chalkboard. Then they select one job from the list to serve as the focus of the interviews to be conducted. (Ten minutes.)

III. Blank paper and pencils are distributed. Concentrating on the chosen job, the participants use brainstorming to make the three determinations emphasized in Step I. During this process the facilitator records the results on newsprint or a chalkboard, inviting the participants to refer to the information throughout the activity. In addition, the participants are encouraged to jot down questions that should be asked of a candidate for the chosen job; it is explained that these questions are for their own use during the activity. (Twenty minutes.)

IV. Triads are formed. Within each triad one member assumes each of the following roles: interviewer, job candidate, and observer. The participants are cautioned to maintain their roles throughout the interviewing process. The interviewer conducts the interview in accordance with information established during Steps I through III; the job candidate responds as required; and the observer makes notes regarding the interviewer's success at finding out what he or she needs to know about the candidate. After the interview the observer provides feedback about the interviewer's performance. (Fifteen minutes.)

V. Within each triad each participant assumes a different role; new interviews are conducted; and the new observer provides feedback. (Fifteen minutes.)

VI. Step V is repeated, with each participant again playing a different role. (Fifteen minutes.)

VII. The total group is reconvened for a concluding discussion. Questions that may be helpful during this discussion are as follows:

1. How did you go about devising questions related to job criteria?
2. What types of questions and techniques seemed to be helpful in eliciting pertinent information? Which were not so successful?
3. When you served as a job candidate, which question or experience carried the greatest impact for you?
4. What conclusions can be drawn about the interview process and the skills that are necessary for the interviewer?
5. How does this activity compare with your own experience as an interviewer? as a job candidate?
6. What is one interviewing skill that you can transfer to your own work environment? In what way might this skill be helpful to you?

Structured Experience   358

Variations

I. New triads may be formed for each round of interviewing.

II. Each triad may choose a job on which to focus.

III. The participants may be given sample job descriptions from which to derive their interviewing questions.

Similar Structured Experiences: *75 Annual:* Structured Experience **142**; *Vol. VII:* **257**; *'83 Annual:* **333**.

Notes on the Use of "Interviewing":

Submitted by Kenneth L. Murrell.

359. THE SALES MANAGER'S JOURNEY: GROUP PROBLEM SOLVING

Goals

    I. To study the sharing of information in a task-oriented group.

    II. To examine the various types of member behavior that emerge as a group works on solving a problem.

Group Size

    One or more groups of five to seven participants each.

Time Required

    One and one-half hours.

Materials

    I. A copy of The Sales Manager's Journey Instruction Sheet for each participant.

    II. A set of information sheets for each group. Each set contains the following:

        1. One copy of The Sales Manager's Journey Information Sheet 1.

        2. One copy of The Sales Manager's Journey Information Sheet 2.

        3. One copy of The Sales Manager's Journey Information Sheet 3.

        4. One copy of The Sales Manager's Journey Information Sheet 4.

        5. One copy of The Sales Manager's Journey Information Sheet 5.

        6. One copy of The Sales Manager's Journey Information Sheet 6 (if needed).

        7. One copy of The Sales Manager's Journey Information Sheet 7 (if needed).

    Note: Sheets 1 through 5 constitute a complete set in that they contain all information necessary to solve the problem involved in the activity; it is essential that all five be distributed to each group. However, Sheets 6 and 7 consist of information duplicated from previous sheets and should be used only when there are more than five participants in a group.

    III. A copy of The Sales Manager's Journey Reaction Form for each participant.

    IV. A copy of The Sales Manager's Journey Solution Sheet for each participant.

    V. A pencil for each participant.

Physical Setting

A room large enough so that the members of each group may sit in a circle and work without disturbing any other groups. Writing surfaces of some type should be provided.

Process

I. The facilitator asks the participants to form groups of five to seven each and requests that the members of each group be seated in a circle.

II. Copies of The Sales Manager's Journey Instruction Sheet are distributed, and the participants are asked to read this handout.

III. A set of information sheets is distributed to each group in such a way that each member receives a different sheet. Pencils are also distributed, and then the groups are instructed to begin their task.

IV. After thirty minutes, even if all groups have not arrived at a solution, the participants are instructed to stop their work. Copies of The Sales Manager's Journey Reaction Form are distributed, and the participants complete this form individually. (Fifteen minutes.)

V. The members of each group are asked to discuss the issues dealt with on the reaction form. (Fifteen minutes.)

VI. The facilitator reassembles the total group, reveals the correct answer *(695 durrs)*, gives a copy of The Sales Manager's Journey Solution Sheet to any participant who wants one, and answers questions about the way in which the solution was derived. The activity concludes with a discussion that focuses on the reaction form and emphasizes the sharing and processing of information in task-oriented groups.

Variations

I. Groups of more than seven participants may be accommodated by creating additional duplicate-information sheets.

II. Competition among groups may be generated and pressure created by announcing that "scores" will be assigned to the groups on the basis of speed and/or accuracy in solving the problem. The following is an example of a point structure that might be used with this approach:

1. Each group starts with 200 points.

2. After ten minutes each group loses 5 points for each additional minute it takes to solve the problem.

3. Any group that reaches an incorrect solution loses 50 points.

4. The first group to arrive at the correct solution is awarded 70 points, the second is awarded 60, the third is awarded 50, and so forth.

III. The facilitator may assist in solving the problem by providing the following hints, either at intervals during the task or in response to incorrect solutions.

1. All of the information you have been given is correct and means precisely what it says.

2. How do you know the route taken by the sales manager?

3. The sales manager may have visited the same town more than once.

IV. The problem may be simplified by removing the redundant and unnecessary facts from the information sheets or by simplifying the route itself.

Similar Structured Experiences: *Vol. II:* Structured Experience **31**; *72 Annual:* **80**; *Vol. IV:* **103, 117**; *74 Annual:* **133**; *Vol. V:* **155, 156**; *76 Annual:* **178**; *'81 Annual:* **284**.

Lecturette Sources: *'73 Annual:* "Conditions Which Hinder Effective Communication"; *'74 Annual:* "Five Components Contributing to Effective Interpersonal Communications."

Notes on the Use of "The Sales Manager's Journey":

This adaptation of "Lutts and Mipps" (*Vol. II*, Structured Experience 31) was submitted by Guy Fielding.

THE SALES MANAGER'S JOURNEY INSTRUCTION SHEET

Lapps, mapps, and *napps* represent a new international distance measurement; similarly, *burrs, currs,* and *durrs* represent a new system of time measurement. The task of your group is to determine as quickly as possible *how many durrs* it took the sales manager for Mighty Micro, a growing electronics firm based in the South, to drive from Town A to Town G. Each group member will be given an information sheet containing part of the data necessary to solve this problem; your group as a whole will have all of the information necessary to solve the problem.

To accomplish this task, you may organize your group in any way you wish. You will probably find that it is more efficient to tell your fellow members the relevant information you have been given than simply to show your data sheet to them.

THE SALES MANAGER'S JOURNEY INFORMATION SHEET 1

1. The road between D and E is a standard, four-lane highway.

2. It took the sales manager 5 currs, 7 durrs to drive from B to D.

3. There are approximately 100 durrs in an hour.

4. There are 5 napps in a mapp.

5. The distance between A and B is 12 napps.

6. The country between A and B is hilly, and the road is narrow and twisting; therefore, progress is generally slow.

7. The distance between F and G is 9 mapps.

8. It took the sales manager 0.9 burrs to drive from C to B.

9. The distance from E to G is 6 mapps.

10. The route between F and G is a cross-country road that is straight, little used, and in good condition.

THE SALES MANAGER'S JOURNEY INFORMATION SHEET 2

1. It is 18 napps from B to C.

2. The sales manager drove from D to E at an average speed of 32 napps per burr.

3. The route between E and F is a recently completed highway.

4. A napp is equal to approximately two kilometers.

5. When the sales manager arrived at E, he had a 45-durr break before continuing.

6. The distance from A to C is 4 mapps, 3 napps.

7. The distance from D to G is 23 napps.

8. A curr is 10 durrs.

9. At an average speed of 30 napps per burr, it took the sales manager 6 currs to drive from B to C.

10. He stopped at C for a 40-durr break.

THE SALES MANAGER'S JOURNEY INFORMATION SHEET 3

1. A durr is 100 frons.

2. A mapp is a measure of distance.

3. It is 18 napps from B to D.

4. After the sales manager arrived at F, he stopped for 6 currs.

5. His average speed on the journey between E and F was 54 napps per burr.

6. The car supplied him by Mighty Micro is a standard American make.

7. The sales manager's average speed while driving from A to B was 24 napps per burr.

8. The distance from C to D is 21 napps.

9. It is 3 mapps, 3 napps from B to C.

10. There is a great deal of heavy, commercial traffic on the road from C to D.

THE SALES MANAGER'S JOURNEY INFORMATION SHEET 4

1. It is 4 mapps, 4 napps from D to E.

2. The sales manager drove from B to C at an average speed of 30 napps per burr.

3. He drove from F to D at 40 napps per burr.

4. He has been traveling this route regularly for the last eighteen months.

5. He stopped at C for 4 currs.

6. It took him 75 durrs to drive from F to D.

7. The road from C to D is usually quite congested, with many heavy trucks using it as a route to railroad centers.

8. The distance from C to E is 7 mapps, 4 napps.

9. The sales manager has been working for Mighty Micro for a little more than two years.

10. The distance from C to D is 21 napps.

THE SALES MANAGER'S JOURNEY INFORMATION SHEET 5

1. A burr is 10 currs.

2. It is 27 napps from E to F.

3. It took the sales manager 9.3 currs to drive from D to G.

4. Because of the work awaiting him at his office, the sales manager was anxious to complete the trip and return as quickly as possible.

5. A lapp is 10 mapps.

6. A burr is a unit of time measurement.

7. Bad weather conditions forced the sales manager to drive more slowly than usual on this trip.

8. While driving from C to B, he was caught in a traffic jam caused by road construction, which delayed him for 20 durrs.

9. It is 30 napps from D to F.

10. It is 45 napps from F to G.

THE SALES MANAGER'S JOURNEY INFORMATION SHEET 6

1. It is 2 mapps, 2 napps from A to B by the shortest route.

2. The sales manager drove from D to E at an average speed of 32 napps per burr.

3. He stopped at E for 45 durrs.

4. It is 18 napps from B to D.

5. Due to bad weather, the overall trip took longer than usual.

6. It took the sales manager 75 durrs to drive from F to D.

7. The route he used on this occasion was his usual one.

8. A curr is 10 durrs.

9. One hour is about 100 durrs.

10. It took the sales manager 0.9 burrs to drive from C to B.

THE SALES MANAGER'S JOURNEY INFORMATION SHEET 7

1. It is 23 napps from A to C.

2. When the sales manager reached F, he had a short break of 60 durrs.

3. While driving from A to B, he averaged 2.4 napps per curr.

4. The road from B to C has been gradually improved over the last few years; bends have been straightened, and the road has been widened. However, construction is still taking place.

5. The route between E and F is almost entirely a four-lane highway.

6. There are 5 napps per mapp.

7. The towns of D and E are 24 napps apart.

8. The sales manager has made rapid progress within the company, and the recent successful marketing of a product referred to as a "Domestic Micro" suggests that another promotion is likely.

9. A napp is a measure of distance.

10. It is 5 mapps, 2 napps from E to F.

THE SALES MANAGER'S JOURNEY REACTION FORM

1. Who participated most in your group?

2. Who participated least?

3. How was participation organized within your group? Who organized it? To whom did the group look for leadership?

4. Which behaviors helped your group to accomplish the task?

5. Which behaviors hindered your group in accomplishing the task? What conflicts emerged?

6. How did your group use the information provided?

7. How did the nature of the information affect the task? the group dynamics?

8. What process did your group follow in solving the problem?

9. If an individual were to tackle this problem alone, how might his or her problem-solving process differ from the process used by your group?

10. If you had to complete another activity of this kind, how could you improve your group's performance?

•

THE SALES MANAGER'S JOURNEY SOLUTION SHEET

The Route Taken

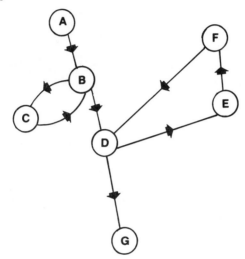

The Solution

Stage	Distance (Napps)	Speed (Napps per Burr)	Time (Durrs)
A to B	12	24	50
B to C	18	30	60
C (pause)	—	—	40
C to B	18	—	90
B to D	18	—	57
D to E	24	32	75
E (pause)	—	—	45
E to F	27	54	50
F (pause)	—	—	60
F to D	30	40	75
D to G	24	—	93
		Total	695

☐ Information to be calculated (formula: time = distance × rate of speed)
— Information not supplied

360. MATRIX: BALANCING ORGANIZATIONAL NEEDS

Goals

    I. To allow the participants to become acquainted with and experience a matrix organizational structure.

    II. To demonstrate the rewards and difficulties experienced by a group that concentrates on task and process simultaneously.

Group Size

    Two or three groups of seven to ten participants each.

Time Required

    Approximately two hours.

Materials

    I. A copy of the Matrix Overview for each participant.

    II. A set of Matrix Role Sheets for each group so that the members may fulfill the following roles:

        1. One corporate-services director;

        2. One personnel director;

        3. One manager; and

        4. Four to seven workers.

    III. Blank paper and a pencil for each participant.

    IV. A clipboard or other portable writing surface for each participant.

    V. A copy of the Matrix Discussion Sheet for each participant.

    VI. A newsprint flip chart and a felt-tipped marker for each group.

Physical Setting

    A large room with movable chairs for the participants. The following diagram shows an arrangement that will accommodate two groups. In each group the workers face a newsprint flip chart.

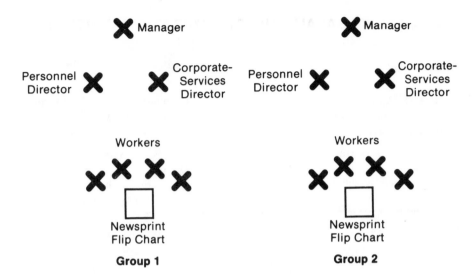

Process

I. The facilitator presents the activity as an introduction to matrix organizations. Each participant is given a copy of the Matrix Overview and is asked to read this handout. Then the facilitator elicits questions about the handout, clarifying as necessary. (Fifteen minutes.)

II. The participants are assembled into two or three groups of seven to ten each. Within each group the facilitator assigns the following roles:

1. One corporate-services director;
2. One personnel director;
3. One manager; and
4. Four to seven workers.

III. Each participant is given a copy of the appropriate role sheet and is instructed to read the sheet. (Five minutes.)

IV. The participants are asked to assume their assigned positions for the beginning of the role play. Each participant is given blank paper, a pencil, and a clipboard or other portable writing surface.

V. After emphasizing that each participant must maintain his or her role until notified otherwise, the facilitator invites the workers in each group to talk quietly among themselves until their manager joins them. Then each group's corporate-services director is asked to begin the activity by meeting with the manager and giving the specified assignment. (Ten minutes.)

VI. Each group's manager is instructed to consult with the personnel director for instructions regarding a different assignment. (Five minutes.)

VII. The manager for each group joins his or her workers, explains the two assignments, asks the workers to begin, and provides whatever assistance is deemed appropriate. As each group works, its directors observe quietly.

VIII. After fifteen minutes the participants are instructed to stop the role play. The facilitator distributes copies of the Matrix Discussion Sheet and asks the members of each group to discuss answers to the questions on this handout. The members are further instructed to select a reporter to record the group's answers and to report later to the total group. (Twenty minutes.)

IX. The total group is reconvened, and the group reporters share the results of the previous step. The facilitator elicits comments from the matrix bosses regarding their observations and then leads a concluding discussion about reactions to and applicability of the matrix concept.

Variations

I. After Step IX two more assignments may be given so that the participants can apply what they have learned.

II. Each matrix boss may be instructed to interrupt the manager whenever his or her specific task is not being worked on.

III. Each worker may be given a group role (for example, a dominator, a harmonizer, or an initiator).

Similar Structured Experience: *Vol. V:* Structured Experience **163**.

Lecturette Sources: *74 Annual:* "Communication Patterns in Organization Structure"; *79 Annual:* "The Systems View of Organizations: Dynamics of Organizational Change"; *'82 Annual:* "Coping with Conflict."

Submitted by James P. Lewis.

Notes on the Use of "Matrix":

MATRIX OVERVIEW

All organizations have two conflicting needs: (a) to attend to the special interests of different parts of the organization and (b) to regulate and integrate all of these parts in harmonious and common action. The matrix organizational structure was devised to address both of these needs. The identifying feature of a matrix organization is that some managers report to two bosses. In such a situation, the two bosses function at the same hierarchical level and are in charge of two related, but different, areas of business, both of which are represented in the subordinate manager's work. This system not only accommodates the special interests of the two areas, but also answers the need for regulation and integration in that both of the bosses report to senior management and both have the same manager or managers one level down reporting to them. A slightly different version frequently occurs in engineering companies, in which two project managers report to the same top executive and have a common pool of engineering professionals working under them and supervised by the manager(s) of that pool.

A simple illustration of a basic matrix system is provided below.

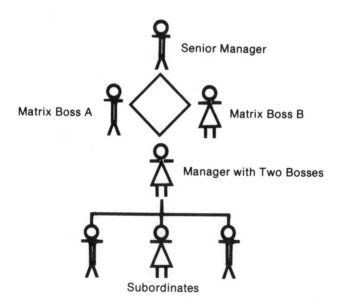

Senior Manager

Matrix Boss A

Matrix Boss B

Manager with Two Bosses

Subordinates

Based on S.M. Davis, "Matrix: Filling the Gap Between Theory and Practice," in W.W. Burke (Ed.), *The Cutting Edge: Current Theory and Practice in Organization Development,* University Associates, 1978.

The Matrix Boss

Each matrix boss is in charge of an entire function, product, area, or service, but is not in total command over the individuals who report to him or her. The matrix boss shares power with an equal, often over the same subordinates and usually over information and issues.

In addition, the matrix boss is required to represent a portion of the organization's activities as well as to maintain an institutional perspective—the corporate point of view. Sharing managerial control is sometimes difficult. The matrix boss must be aware that his or her subordinates have other voices to listen to and other priorities. Great care must be taken to ensure that the logic behind and importance of any directives are clear.

The Manager with Two Bosses

The way to be successful as a manager with two bosses is to accept the fact that although contradictory demands may be made, the matrix system is the best way to accommodate simultaneous and/or competing organizational needs. When viewed from this perspective, the manager's role really is not so different from that of the traditional manager; in both cases attention must be paid to competing demands, tradeoffs, and conflicts. However, when this perspective is not assumed or when the matrix system functions poorly, the manager may become preoccupied with internal issues. Ultimately, the result may be a feeling that the organization lacks direction.

MATRIX ROLE SHEET

Matrix Boss: Corporate-Services Director

You are the corporate-services director for an organization that is in a state of transition. The organization has grown very rapidly during the past two years, and this growth has generated a number of problems. In an attempt to resolve these problems, top management has just named you the chairperson of a task force that has been charged with determining actions to take toward resolving internal turmoil. You have also been told that the first meeting of the task force is today and that you must come to the meeting with some data that will serve as a starting point.

One of the departments under your supervision is responsible for analyzing corporate processes and making suggestions for their improvement. You feel that the members of this department will be essential to the completion of this task and that they can provide you with the data you need for today's meeting. Thus, after some thought, you have decided to explain the task to the department manager and to request that the department members contribute their ideas about *the five major characteristics of each of the following:*

- *Effective interpersonal relations in a work group;*
- *Effective problem solving in a work group;*
- *An effective worker; and*
- *An effective manager.*

You realize that you will need time to assess the results of the assignment before you attend the task-force meeting. Thus, you plan to ask the manager to have the department members complete the assignment in fifteen minutes.

After the manager joins his or her workers, you should move close to the group and observe quietly.

MATRIX ROLE SHEET

Matrix Boss: Personnel Director

You are the personnel director for an organization that is in a state of transition. As a result of recent growth, the organization has found it increasingly difficult to maintain its commitment to human resource development. In an attempt to resolve this problem, top management has just named you the chairperson of a task force that has been charged with establishing a new program for human resource development. You have also been told that the first meeting of the task force is today and that you must come to the meeting with some data that will serve as a starting point.

One of the departments under your supervision is responsible for analyzing corporate processes and making suggestions for their improvement. You feel that the members of this department will be essential to the completion of this task and that they can provide you with the data you need for today's meeting. Thus, after some thought, you have decided to explain the task to the department manager and to request that the department members contribute their ideas about *ten ways in which managers can foster participation and involvement among their subordinates.*

You realize that you will need time to assess the results of the assignment before you attend the task-force meeting. Thus, you plan to ask the manager to have the department members complete the assignment in fifteen minutes.

After the manager joins his or her workers, you should move close to the group and observe quietly.

MATRIX ROLE SHEET

Manager

You are the manager of a department that analyzes corporate processes and makes suggestions for their improvement. You report to two matrix bosses: the corporate-services director and the personnel director.

During this activity you will be given an assignment by each of these bosses. It is your responsibility to ensure that both assignments are completed. You will need to explain the assignments to your subordinates and provide any clarifying information and help that they require.

After you have received the assignments, you will have *fifteen minutes* to explain, delegate, supervise, and follow through to completion. You may use any supervisory methods that you feel are appropriate. A newsprint flip chart and a felt-tipped marker will be provided.

MATRIX ROLE SHEET

Worker

You are a worker in a department that analyzes corporate processes and makes suggestions for their improvement. The organization that employs you operates within a matrix structure. The manager of your department, who is your direct supervisor, reports to two matrix bosses: the corporate-services director and the personnel director.

During this activity you will be given instructions by your manager. These instructions are the result of two different assignments, one from each director, that must be completed concurrently and within a time limit. Your manager will provide the details. Do your best to comply with all instructions.

MATRIX DISCUSSION SHEET

1. How did the manager feel about each assignment?

2. How did the manager's approach to the assignments help or hinder their completion? How did this approach help or hinder the workers' morale?

3. How did the manager and the workers feel about having to complete two assignments simultaneously? Did one assignment assume precedence over the other? If so, why?

4. What were the positive effects of having to complete both assignments within the specified time limit? What were the negative effects?

5. What might be some of the benefits and pitfalls inherent within a matrix system?

6. Would a matrix structure work within your own organization? Why or why not?

361. VALUES AND DECISIONS: CHECKING FOR CONGRUENCE

Goals

    I. To help the participants to clarify their personal values.

    II. To explore the relationship between the participants' values and their major life decisions.

    III. To identify factors that affect commitment to values in decision making.

Group Size

    Any number of triads.

Time Required

    One hour and forty-five minutes.

Materials

    I. A copy of the Values and Decisions Work Sheet for each participant.

    II. A copy of the Values and Decisions Matrix Sheet for each participant.

    III. A pencil for each participant.

    IV. A newsprint flip chart and a felt-tipped marker or a chalkboard and chalk.

Physical Setting

    A room that will accommodate all participants in triads. A writing surface should be provided for each participant.

Process

    I. The facilitator introduces the activity as one that will explore how values affect decisions. Then each participant is given a copy of the Values and Decisions Work Sheet and a pencil and is asked to complete the work sheet. (Fifteen minutes.)

    II. The facilitator distributes the Values and Decisions Matrix Sheets and instructs each participant to list on the sheet his or her three most important life decisions (that is, decisions that have shaped the person's current situation or circumstances). (Ten minutes.)

III. The participants are directed to list their highest ranked values, both espoused and rejected, on their matrix sheets. (Five minutes.)

IV. The facilitator gives the following instructions:

1. Evaluate the first life decision horizontally across the matrix; for each square associated with a particular value, determine whether the decision made was congruent with (or served to advance) that value. If so, enter a plus sign (+) in the square.

2. If the decision did not serve to advance the value or was contrary to it, enter a minus sign (-) in the square.

3. If there seems to be *no* relationship between the decision and the value, enter a zero (0) in the square.

4. Repeat this procedure for the other life decisions in relation to each of the six values listed.

(Five minutes.)

V. The participants form triads to compare their results and to discuss any incongruence between their decisions and their stated values and how they feel about it. (Twenty minutes.)

VI. The facilitator posts the following questions on newsprint or a chalkboard and directs the triads to consider them:

1. Were there more pluses, minuses, or zeros on the members' matrix sheets? What does this information suggest?

2. Are any general patterns apparent in all the matrix sheets? If so, what are they?

3. How committed are the members to decisions that were in accordance with their stated values? How committed are they to decisions that were in conflict with or not related to their stated values?

4. What does the experience imply about values that are acted on versus values that are espoused or rejected?

(Twenty minutes.)

VII. The total group is reconvened, and the facilitator guides the participants in discussing what was learned from the experience. The following questions may be included in this discussion:

1. What happens when a person makes decisions that bear no relation to his or her values?

2. What happens when a person makes decisions that are incongruous with his or her stated values?

3. What implications do these matters have for the further examination of one's values?

4. What implications do these matters have for making important decisions about one's life and work?

5. What can one do to ensure that one's decisions are congruent with one's values?

(Fifteen minutes.)

VIII. The triads are reassembled or new triads are formed, and the members discuss ways in which they can utilize this approach to guide their future decisions.

Variations

I. The facilitator may begin the activity with a brief lecturette on the theory of value clarification and its relevance to the group's purpose.

II. Subgroups of two or four participants each may be substituted for the triads.

III. The triads formed during Step V may be retained throughout a training event so that the data generated can be used as the basis for guiding feedback on members' behavior during the event.

IV. During Step VI the facilitator may obtain data from the triads in order to generate a group profile of the relationship between the members' espoused values and their life decisions. Implications of these results are then processed during Step VII.

V. The facilitator may use a different work sheet that focuses on values that are more specific to the group involved (for example, work values, health values, or relationship values).

Similar Structured Experiences: *Vol. II:* Structured Experience **46**; *'73 Annual:* **94**; *'75 Annual:* **143**; *'79 Annual:* **233**; *Vol. VIII:* **298**; *'82 Annual:* **321**.

Suggested Instruments: *Vol. III:* "Intentions and Choices Inventory"; *'74 Annual:* "Self-Disclosure Questionnaire"; *'78 Annual:* "Mach V Attitude Inventory"; *'82 Annual:* "Life-Style Questionnaire."

Lecturette Source: *'81 Annual:* "Intrapersonal Conflict Resolution."

Submitted by Gib Akin.

Notes on the Use of "Values and Decisions":

VALUES AND DECISIONS WORK SHEET

Instructions: Enter a check mark (✓) beside each value that you personally espouse and enter an X beside each that you personally reject. Then rank order the three values that you hold most strongly; write the number 1 beside your pre-eminent value, 2 by the second most strongly held, and 3 by the third. Finally, in the same manner, rank order the three that you reject most strongly.

It is valuable to:

———— Get ahead.

———— Be honest.

———— Participate in government.

———— Work hard.

———— Be clean.

———— Honor one's parents.

———— Be loyal to one's country.

———— Live.

———— Be free.

———— Pursue happiness.

———— Accrue goods and wealth.

———— Become educated.

———— Be religious.

———— Know the right people.

———— Live in the right place.

———— Be productive.

———— Help one's fellow man.

———— Be tolerant.

———— Explore.

———— Win.

———— Look out for oneself.

———— Obey the law.

———— Influence other countries to become democratic.

———— Be partisan.

———— Know one's heritage.

———— Build things.

———— Save time.

———— Find a better way.

———— Be proud of one's city, state, and region.

———— Adjust to the prevailing social norms.

———— Stand up for what one thinks is right.

Adapted from Traditional American Values Worksheet, in J.E. Jones and J.W. Pfeiffer (Eds.), *The 1973 Annual Handbook for Group Facilitators*, p. 25, University Associates, 1973.

VALUES AND DECISIONS MATRIX SHEET

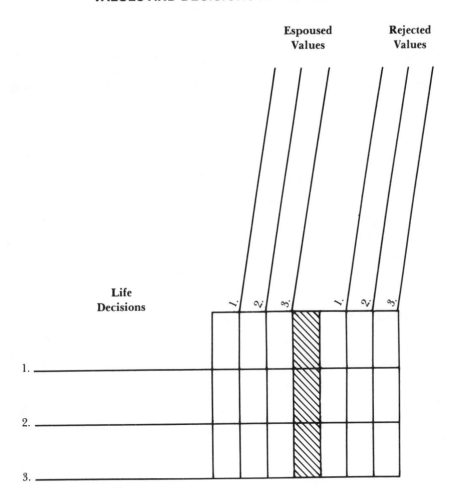

362. THE PROMOTION: VALUE CLARIFICATION

Goals

   I. To provide an opportunity for the participants to practice identifying and clarifying values.

   II. To help the participants to become aware of some of the factors that affect their own value judgments as well as those of others.

Group Size

   Any number of groups of five to seven participants each.

Time Required

   Two hours and fifteen minutes.

Materials

   I. A copy of The Promotion Case-History Sheet for each participant.

   II. A pencil for each participant.

   III. A sheet of newsprint and a felt-tipped marker for each group.

   IV. Masking tape for each group.

   V. Newsprint and a felt-tipped marker or a chalkboard and chalk (for the facilitator's use).

Physical Setting

   A room large enough to accommodate all groups. During Step II each group should be placed near a wall so that a sheet of newsprint can be displayed within the view of all of its members.

Process

   I. The facilitator introduces the activity and its goals.

   II. The participants are assembled into groups of five to seven each and are given copies of The Promotion Case-History Sheet and pencils.

III. The facilitator asks the participants to read the case-history sheet and to follow the instructions at the end of the handout. (Fifteen minutes.)

IV. The members of each group are instructed to share their rankings, disclosing their rationales and articulating their associated values and beliefs as clearly as possible. It is emphasized that during this sharing no one is to express an opinion regarding another member's decisions or beliefs; requests for clarification are the only permissible comments. (Fifteen minutes.)

V. Each group is given a sheet of newsprint, a felt-tipped marker, and masking tape. The facilitator explains that the members of each group are to try to reach a consensus regarding the ranking of any or all of the characters. If such a consensus is reached, one member should be appointed to record the group's decisions on newsprint and post the newsprint; if no consensus is possible, nothing is posted. (Twenty minutes.)

VI. The facilitator writes the following questions on newsprint or a chalkboard, explaining that each group is to incorporate them into a discussion of reactions to the activity.

  1. What values seemed to underlie the choices that were made?
  2. What similarities in members' values became apparent? What differences became apparent? How do you account for the similarities and differences?
  3. What statements can be made about the effects of values on decisions? on conduct at work?

  (Twenty minutes.)

VII. The total group is reconvened for sharing of answers to the questions posted during the previous step. (Ten minutes.)

VIII. New groups of three or four participants each are assembled. Each participant is asked to identify and discuss with fellow group members one or two significant factors that influence his or her judgment in similar situations that involve value conflicts. (Fifteen minutes.)

IX. A volunteer from each group reports to the total group on typical factors that were identified during the previous step. (Ten minutes.)

X. The facilitator summarizes the general themes expressed in the group reports and then elicits comments from the participants regarding possible applications of their learnings.

Variations

I. To shorten the activity, Steps VIII and IX may be eliminated. In Step X the participants may be asked to make statements about back-home applications.

II. The activity may be altered to focus more on the sexual issues involved. In this case the following goals are applicable:

1. To promote awareness of the complexity of human sexuality as a factor of influence in an organizational setting.

2. To provide an opportunity for the participants to examine their own values and beliefs about the expression of sexuality in organizations.

Changes also should be made in the process. In Steps III, IV, and V, the participants may be asked to determine what Carol should do and then discuss these decisions in their groups, revealing their rationales and trying to achieve a group consensus on this matter.

Subsequently, Steps VI through X may be deleted and the following substitutions made:

VI. The total group is reconvened, and the facilitator requests that a volunteer spokesperson from each group report any consensus achieved.

VII. The individual groups are reassembled, and the members of each group are asked to discuss their reactions to the entire activity and to consider the various ways in which sexuality is expressed in organizations. The facilitator writes the following questions on newsprint or a chalkboard, explaining that each group is to incorporate them into its discussion.

1. How is sexuality expressed in organizations?

2. Which expressions of sexuality are permissible? Which are not permissible?

3. When sexuality is expressed within an organization, what are the positive effects on organizational members? What are the negative effects?

4. What if the sexes were reversed for the characters in the case history? What differences might such reversals make?

(Twenty minutes.)

VIII. After reconvening the total group, the facilitator leads a discussion of the range of values, beliefs, and choices that emerged during the previous step.

Similar Structured Experiences: *Vol. V:* Structured Experience **158**; *Vol. VI:* **215**; *'79 Annual:* **235**; *Vol. VII:* **258**: *'80 Annual:* **272**; *'81 Annual:* **283**.

Suggested Instruments: *Vol. III:* "Polarization: Opinionnaire on Womanhood"; *73 Annual:* "Sex-Role Stereotyping Rating Scale"; *77 Annual:* "Bem Sex-Role Inventory (BSRI)"; *79 Annual:* "Women as Managers Scale (WAMS)"; *Vol. VII:* "Sexual Values in Organizations Questionnaire."

Lecturette Source: *'77 Annual:* "Androgyny."

Notes on the Use of "The Promotion":

Submitted by Janet Lee Mills. A previous version of this structured experience was published in *Developments in Business Simulation & Experiential Exercises,* Vol. 8, the proceedings of the Eighth Annual Conference of the Association for Business Simulation and Experiential Learning (ABSEL), William D. Biggs and David J. Fritzsche (Eds.), copyright © 1980, ABSEL, pp. 1-3. This version, which is also an adaptation of "Louisa's Problem" (*'81 Annual,* Structured Experience 283), is used with the permission of ABSEL.

THE PROMOTION CASE-HISTORY SHEET

Background

Carol was a bright, ambitious woman who held an M.B.A. and until recently had set her sights on a managerial career with Benton Electronics, Inc. She was eager to climb the ladder of success and was willing to work very hard for her promotions. Carol realized that she worked in a highly competitive organization and that she was in a field traditionally dominated by men. Furthermore, she had observed that many men and women never progressed beyond certain rungs of the corporate ladder and that only one woman in the company had entered into top management. Carol knew from the outset that many tests of her ability and loyalty were to come, but she was eager to meet them.

One obstacle to Carol's career at Benton was her exclusion from some informal networks within the organization. Another problem was that although many men seemed to have special sponsors or mentors who "taught them the ropes" and provided them with inside information, she had no such affiliation. However, because she was determined, she attended every seminar she could and lunched regularly with her peers, most of whom were men. Over time she came to trust a co-worker named *Pat*; the two shared confidences frequently and provided valuable feedback to each other regarding work-related matters. Carol valued Pat as a trusted colleague and a friend.

Bob, Carol's supervisor, also had his sights set on top management. He was in the upper echelon of middle management and had made many friends and a few enemies in the company. At the time of the incidents in question, he was in his mid-forties and had been re-examining his goals and values because of a personal crisis: His wife was suing him for divorce, claiming he had neglected her and their children in his "workaholic pursuit of career." Lonely, confused, and in need of comfort, Bob began seeking a confidant, someone who would be supportive and patient and provide a listening ear. Eventually he gravitated toward Carol to fill this role. Only a year before, though, he had felt ambivalent about hiring Carol, assuming that sooner or later she would marry, become pregnant, and resign.

While Bob was in his state of depression, he alternately threw himself relentlessly into his work (at which time Carol's loyalty was evident in her overtime efforts) or dawdled away his time preoccupied with personal problems and the search for "some values of substance" (at which time Carol and Pat tended to cover for him). On one occasion when Bob returned from lunch less than sober, Carol volunteered to attend a meeting in his place.

John, one of the company's several vice presidents, took an immediate interest in Carol when he met her at the meeting she attended in place of Bob. He saw her as both a capable middle manager and a lovely woman. Their acquaintance grew, and Carol gained a great deal of informal knowledge about the company from John's casual conversations. She learned, among other things, that Bob had "locked horns" with John on an issue some years ago and that subsequently the two had been, for all practical purposes, unfriendly. She also learned that Bob's unsteady performance was under close scrutiny and that his transfer to a parallel position in a regional office was imminent. John's advances toward Carol continued and became romantic. Although she was not involved with another man and she would have preferred to keep her relationship with John a business one, she yielded to her own sexual needs and John's steady pursuit. They became lovers.

Eventually Carol confided in Pat, describing both the romance and the wealth of informal knowledge she was gaining. She was not prepared for Pat's abrupt response: "I don't know what to say. Frankly, I wish it were me." Carol was taken aback and began feeling very uneasy around Pat. Consequently, a distance grew between them.

Within a week of Carol's conversation with Pat, Bob called Carol into his office and confronted her with the rumor he had heard that she was sleeping with at least one of the company's vice presidents. He asked her to verify the rumor or deny it. Under pressure, Carol took the stance that her private life was her own. Bob said that he interpreted her comment to be an admission of guilt and fired her with one month's notice. Her appeal to his sense of fairness was of no avail; he replied that her involvement was a serious breach of loyalty that damaged her credibility irreparably.

Stunned, Carol sought the support of John, who said he was helpless to do anything on her behalf under the circumstances. Nonetheless, he promised continuing emotional support and said he hoped that the situation would not interfere with their relationship. Her former friend and confidant, Pat, suggested that she leave the company quietly and not create a public stir through Affirmative Action. Her lawyer, although willing to take the case, advised her similarly, "The best time to find a job is while you have one."

Carol's alternatives seemed bleak indeed when *Joe*, director of another division in the company, heard about the incident and called her to his office. Joe began by briefing Carol on his understanding of recent events, indicating that he was aware of her good work and that he felt her dismissal was unreasonable. He reported that Bob's transfer was now fact, that Pat had been appointed as his replacement, and that Carol had been among those considered for the position before her dismissal. Joe shook his head sadly and said that he had been an advocate of "free sex" for years. He then told Carol that he was willing to create a position for her in his office in light of her record and that this position would be equivalent in rank to the one she had just lost. He also suggested that a couple of years of experience in his division would greatly enhance her career.

Carol left Joe's office with mixed feelings; she felt a rapport with Joe and sensed that they would get along, but she was not sure that she trusted his warmth and generosity. She wondered whether there was innuendo in his offer, whether she was being placated by the organization in some way, whether she could discern the real situation, and whether any of these things even mattered.

Instructions

Rank order the following characters from *1* (least objectionable) to 5 (most objectionable):

_____ Carol

_____ Pat

_____ Bob

_____ John

_____ Joe

363. TRAINING PHILOSOPHIES: A PERSONAL ASSESSMENT

Goals

I. To assist the participants in clarifying their individual training philosophies.

II. To help the participants to clarify their perceptions of the relationship between training and management.

Group Size

Any number of groups of three to four participants each.

Time Required

One hour.

Materials

I. A copy of the Training Philosophies Profile for each participant.

II. A copy of the Training Philosophies Score Sheet for each participant.

III. A copy of the Training Philosophies Interpretation Sheet for each participant.

IV. A pencil for each participant.

Physical Setting

A room with movable chairs for the participants.

Process

I. The facilitator distributes copies of the Training Philosophies Profile and pencils and asks each participant to complete the form. (Fifteen minutes.)

II. The facilitator distributes copies of the Training Philosophies Score Sheet and asks each participant to score his or her profile and to note the philosophy that corresponds to the highest score. (Five minutes.)

III. Each participant is given a copy of the Training Philosophies Interpretation Sheet and is asked to read this handout. Subsequently, the facilitator leads a discussion about the philosophies dealt with in the profile. The following questions may be helpful during this discûssion:

1. What did the profile reveal about your training philosophy? How do you feel about your discoveries?
2. What type of philosophy do you see as predominant in your organization? with trainers in general?
3. What might be the result of each of the underlying attitudes? How can each be used productively?
4. How can you work to change training philosophies for the better?

(Twenty minutes.)

IV. The participants are assembled into groups of three or four each and are invited to discuss how they feel about their scores and the implications of what they have learned.

Variations

I. After Step II each participant may be asked to predict his or her highest-scored philosophy.

II. The participants may be asked to compare their own training philosophies with those of their organizations.

III. The facilitator may request that the group choose an "ideal" philosophy and discuss ways of acting in accordance with that philosophy.

Similar Structured Experience: *Vol. I:* Structured Experience **24**.

Suggested Instruments: *79 Annual:* "Training Style Inventory (TSI)"; *'80 Annual:* "Role Efficacy Scale."

Lecturette Sources: *'72 Annual:* "Risk-Taking and Error Protection Styles"; *'80 Annual:* "Dimensions of Role Efficacy."

Submitted by G.E.H. Beamish.

Notes on the Use of "Training Philosophies":

TRAINING PHILOSOPHIES PROFILE

Instructions: For each of the following thirty-six pairs of statements, allocate 3 points between the alternatives. Make your determination by deciding which of the two better describes how you feel about training. All 3 points must be allocated, but any distribution from 3-0 to 0-3 is permitted. Only whole points may be allocated. (*Note:* This instrument consists of nine different sentences that are repeated throughout in different combinations to form the pairs.)

1.	A	Training makes a valuable contribution to effective management, and this contribution can be clearly demonstrated.
	B	Training makes little difference, but it can be a rewarding job if the trainer deals with acceptable subjects.
2.	C	Training could really put some people right, but those who could benefit most do not risk taking part.
	D	Training has little contribution to make to management; the real action is outside the field of training.
3.	E	Training is not yet perfect, but trainers come closer to the final answer with each new idea.
	F	Training should not move faster than the organization; it should be accomplished step by step.
4.	G	Training seldom changes anything directly, but the trainer who knows the system can stay ahead of the game.
	H	Training consists of finding ways to open up the organization and thereby make it more effective.

5.	I	Training is not about methods; it is about changing and learning to cope with change.
	A	Training makes a valuable contribution to effective management, and this contribution can be clearly demonstrated.
6.	B	Training makes little difference, but it can be a rewarding job if the trainer deals with acceptable subjects.
	C	Training could really put some people right, but those who could benefit most do not risk taking part.
7.	D	Training has little contribution to make to management; the real action is outside the field of training.
	E	Training is not yet perfect, but trainers come closer to the final answer with each new idea.
8.	F	Training should not move faster than the organization; it should be accomplished step by step.
	G	Training seldom changes anything directly, but the trainer who knows the system can stay ahead of the game.
9.	H	Training consists of finding ways to open up the organization and thereby make it more effective.
	I	Training is not about methods; it is about changing and learning to cope with change.
10.	A	Training makes a valuable contribution to effective management, and this contribution can be clearly demonstrated.
	C	Training could really put some people right, but those who could benefit most do not risk taking part.

11.	B	Training makes little difference, but it can be a rewarding job if the trainer deals with acceptable subjects.
	D	Training has little contribution to make to management; the real action is outside the field of training.
12.	E	Training is not yet perfect, but trainers come closer to the final answer with each new idea.
	G	Training seldom changes anything directly, but the trainer who knows the system can stay ahead of the game.
13.	F	Training should not move faster than the organization; it should be accomplished step by step.
	H	Training consists of finding ways to open up the organization and thereby make it more effective.
14.	G	Training seldom changes anything directly, but the trainer who knows the system can stay ahead of the game.
	I	Training is not about methods; it is about changing and learning to cope with change.
15.	C	Training could really put some people right, but those who could benefit most do not risk taking part.
	E	Training is not yet perfect, but trainers come closer to the final answer with each new idea.
16.	D	Training has little contribution to make to management; the real action is outside the field of training.
	F	Training should not move faster than the organization; it should be accomplished step by step.

17.	A	Training makes a valuable contribution to effective management, and this contribution can be clearly demonstrated.
	D	Training has little contribution to make to management; the real action is outside the field of training.
18.	B	Training makes little difference, but it can be a rewarding job if the trainer deals with acceptable subjects.
	E	Training is not yet perfect, but trainers come closer to the final answer with each new idea.
19.	C	Training could really put some people right, but those who could benefit most do not risk taking part.
	F	Training should not move faster than the organization; it should be accomplished step by step.
20.	D	Training has little contribution to make to management; the real action is outside the field of training.
	G	Training seldom changes anything directly, but the trainer who knows the system can stay ahead of the game.
21.	E	Training is not yet perfect, but trainers come closer to the final answer with each new idea.
	H	Training consists of finding ways to open up the organization and thereby make it more effective.
22.	F	Training should not move faster than the organization; it should be accomplished step by step.
	I	Training is not about methods; it is about changing and learning to cope with change.

23.	A	Training makes a valuable contribution to effective management, and this contribution can be clearly demonstrated.
	E	Training is not yet perfect, but trainers come closer to the final answer with each new idea.
24.	B	Training makes little difference, but it can be a rewarding job if the trainer deals with acceptable subjects.
	F	Training should not move faster than the organization; it should be accomplished step by step.
25.	C	Training could really put some people right, but those who could benefit most do not risk taking part.
	G	Training seldom changes anything directly, but the trainer who knows the system can stay ahead of the game.
26.	D	Training has little contribution to make to management; the real action is outside the field of training.
	H	Training consists of finding ways to open up the organization and thereby make it more effective.
27.	E	Training is not yet perfect, but trainers come closer to the final answer with each new idea.
	I	Training is not about methods; it is about changing and learning to cope with change.
28.	A	Training makes a valuable contribution to effective management, and this contribution can be clearly demonstrated.
	F	Training should not move faster than the organization; it should be accomplished step by step.

29.	B	Training makes little difference, but it can be a rewarding job if the trainer deals with acceptable subjects.
	G	Training seldom changes anything directly, but the trainer who knows the system can stay ahead of the game.
30.	C	Training could really put some people right, but those who could benefit most do not risk taking part.
	H	Training consists of finding ways to open up the organization and thereby make it more effective.
31.	D	Training has little contribution to make to management; the real action is outside the field of training.
	I	Training is not about methods; it is about changing and learning to cope with change.
32.	A	Training makes a valuable contribution to effective management, and this contribution can be clearly demonstrated.
	G	Training seldom changes anything directly, but the trainer who knows the system can stay ahead of the game.
33.	B	Training makes little difference, but it can be a rewarding job if the trainer deals with acceptable subjects.
	H	Training consists of finding ways to open up the organization and thereby make it more effective.
34.	C	Training could really put some people right, but those who could benefit most do not risk taking part.
	I	Training is not about methods; it is about changing and learning to cope with change.

35.	A	Training makes a valuable contribution to effective management, and this contribution can be clearly demonstrated.
	H	Training consists of finding ways to open up the organization and thereby make it more effective.
36.	B	Training makes little difference, but it can be a rewarding job if the trainer deals with acceptable subjects.
	I	Training is not about methods; it is about changing and learning to cope with change.

TRAINING PHILOSOPHIES SCORE SHEET

For each of the letters A through I, total the number of points and enter the result in the appropriate box. The grand total of all scores should be 108.

A   B   C   D   E   F   G   H   I

$$\Box + \Box + \Box + \Box + \Box + \Box + \Box + \Box + \Box = 108$$

The letters A through I represent philosophies as follows:

- A - Justification
- B - Rationalization
- C - Cynicism
- D - Escapism
- E - Miracle seeking
- F - Pragmatism
- G - Political expedience
- H - Pursuit of learning
- I - Achievement integration

TRAINING PHILOSOPHIES INTERPRETATION SHEET

Philosophy	Behavior	Self-Image	Underlying Attitude
A. Justification	Denies that there is anything wrong with training. Conducts evaluations and cites validations to prove this point	Teacher who battles against ignorance	People will eventually recognize the contributions of trainers.
B. Rationalization	Deals only with "safe" subjects; does not "rock the boat"	Teacher who is trying to avoid personal burnout	Training is easy if the trainer maintains a low profile.
C. Cynicism	Uses training to punish others or to belittle them for their naivete	Clinical observer who understands people's hidden motives	Training could "save" everyone, but people do not deserve it or recognize its value.
D. Escapism	Leaves the profession	Expert who is too good to waste on a useless or unrewarding occupation	There is no real future for trainers.
E. Miracle seeking	Earnestly seeks the ultimate answer; open to evangelistic fads	Messiah (designate)	All uncertainty about training will be resolved when the right technique is discovered.

Philosophy	Behavior	Self-Image	Underlying Attitude
F. Pragmatism	Makes changes that people will tolerate	Change agent who achieves progress in small increments	Slow but steady improvement is possible through training.
G. Political expedience	Works the system, usually to his or her personal advantage	Shrewd manipulator	If and when training changes things for the better, the improvement will help me.
H. Pursuit of learning	Seeks ways to improve effectiveness	Honest and open seeker of wisdom and truth	Training can improve organizations by showing people how to pull together.
I. Achievement integration	Promotes change, sometimes without knowing how	Mover	Organizations are changing, and training teaches people how to cope with change.

364. AIRSOPAC: CHOOSING A CEO

Goals

I. To explore values in executive decision making.

II. To allow the participants to study procedures used by groups to evaluate individual differences among highly qualified people.

III. To examine the impact of individual values and attitudes on group decision making.

Group Size

Any number of groups of five to nine participants each.

Time Required

Two to two and one-half hours.

Materials

I. A copy of the AIRSOPAC Information Sheet for each participant.

II. A copy of the AIRSOPAC Discussion Sheet for each participant.

III. Blank paper and a pencil for each spokesperson.

IV. A clipboard or other portable writing surface for each spokesperson.

Physical Setting

A room large enough so that the groups can work without disturbing one another. Chairs should be provided.

Process

I. The facilitator briefly discusses the goals of the activity and then forms groups of five to nine participants each.

II. Each participant is given a copy of the information sheet and is asked to read this handout. After all participants have finished reading, the facilitator elicits and answers questions about the task, clarifying that each group is to act as a separate board of directors and emphasizing that the members must reach a consensus regarding the CEO and an alternate. Then the groups are told that their time limit is forty-five minutes and are instructed to begin.

III. After forty-five minutes the facilitator asks the groups to stop their work, distributes copies of the discussion sheet, and asks the members of each group to answer the questions on this sheet. Each group is also instructed to select a spokesperson to record the group's answers and to report these answers later to the total group. Blank paper, a pencil, and a clipboard or other portable writing surface are given to each group for the spokesperson's use. (Thirty minutes.)

IV. The total group is reconvened, and the spokespersons are asked to take turns reporting their groups' answers.

V. The facilitator leads a concluding discussion.

Variations

I. The facilitator may begin the activity with a lecturette on value clarification and/or consensus tasks.

II. The candidate data may be revised to add or delete variables, or specific candidates may be added or deleted.

III. The decision-making process may be emphasized more strongly.

IV. With individual groups of seven, the activity may be used as a role play in which each of the members not only serves on the board of directors but also assumes the role of one of the candidates.

Similar Structured Experiences: *Vol. IV:* Structured Experience **106**; *'74 Annual:* **127**, **135**; *'83 Annual:* **340**.

Suggested Instrument: *'79 Annual:* "Women as Managers Scale (WAMS)."

Lecturette Sources: *73 Annual:* "Synergy and Consensus-Seeking"; *79 Annual:* "Anybody with Eyes Can See the Facts!"

Submitted by Thomas H. Patten, Jr.

Notes on the Use of "AIRSOPAC":

AIRSOPAC INFORMATION SHEET

AIRSOPAC is a successful airline that was founded in the United States. Its 105 aircraft make 725 daily flights and serve ninety-eight cities and locales in California, Oregon, Washington, Hawaii, Micronesia, and Melanesia, including such exotic destinations as Tahiti, Tonga, and Fiji as well as Papua, New Guinea; Auckland, New Zealand; and Sydney, Australia. AIRSOPAC uses airports at three locations as "hubs": Ontario, California (near Los Angeles); Honolulu; and American Samoa.

Over the next decade the airline plans to replace its present fleet of aircraft with new, fuel-efficient Boeing 767s and DeHavilands. This program will cost almost one billion dollars during the first phase of implementation, which is scheduled to end in 1989.

The airline also plans to extend service by 1992 to Singapore, Kuala Lumpur, Jakarta, Manila, Shanghai, and Tokyo. The new aircraft to be ordered will make it technically possible to extend the service. However, a myriad of details concerning legal, financial, marketing, operational, political, and international issues must be thought through before the extension can become a reality. The satisfactory completion of this planning and its implementation are a challenging task for top management, particularly in an environment in which financing is difficult to obtain and competition for customers is fierce. The picture is further complicated by the existence of foreign-government-owned airlines that fly to various destinations that AIRSOPAC services or plans to service.

The chief executive officer (CEO) of AIRSOPAC retires in ninety days after thirty-five years with the company. A group of seven possible replacements from within the corporation has been identified by the board of directors. The issue of replacement has been studied for a long time, and now that all the important facts are at hand, a decision is imminent.

You are a member of the board of directors. The board's immediate task is to choose the next CEO, who will have the title of president. The chairman of the board at AIRSOPAC deals strictly with matters of long-range policy and relationships with the financial committee of the board of directors. Therefore, the CEO must be someone who can marshal the human and other resources of AIRSOPAC so that its mission for the future will be fulfilled. In the process of choosing the CEO, the board must also identify that person's most likely replacement, who would serve as an interim president in the event that the CEO died suddenly or was temporarily incapacitated. The board members' choices of a CEO and an alternate must be unanimous. Another important point to keep in mind is that the company has had a good record in equal-employment opportunity and affirmative action, although it has attained this record only through great effort on the part of top management.

There are seven candidates for the position of CEO. These individuals, whose biographical sketches follow, are long-service managerial employees of the company. Each has the present rank of vice president of a division or a staff department. They are peers. All have had distinguished records of performance in recent years and successful overall careers to date.

1. Robert K. Andrews

Sixty-year-old white male. Career pattern is balanced among marketing, finance, operations, and high-level general management. B.A., University of California at Los Angeles. Married. Three grown children, one of whom is a leader in the San Francisco homosexual community. Recently bought a second home in Tucson. Health is excellent. Under consideration for a Cabinet position in Washington as Secretary of Commerce. Built and possesses a famous collection of Oriental postage stamps. Considered an outstanding, well-rounded manager with high leadership qualifications. Has no corporate enemies and much subordinate support. Keeps his political views to himself. Twenty-five years in the company.

2. Harold R. Bennett

Thirty-nine-year-old white male. Career as an aerospace engineer, a successful airline entrepreneur, and a general manager. B.S., Cornell; M.S., Massachusetts Institute of Technology. Divorced twice. Five children under fifteen years of age. Occasionally becomes extremely intoxicated off the job. Won the Congressional Medal of Honor in Vietnam. Active in the National Rifle Association and the Republican Party's conservative wing. Founded and was CEO of a very financially successful interisland airline in Hawaii that was bought out by AIRSOPAC and absorbed in the late Seventies. Very popular and well liked. Ten years in the company.

3. Franklin Cavender

Forty-two-year-old black male. Career as a financial and strategic planner with four years of exposure to operations at the Ontario "hub." B.A., Fisk; M.B.A., Harvard Business School. Married. Two teenage daughters. Likes motorcycles. Has not had a health examination for five years, but has no apparent problems. Wife is a television newscaster with a national reputation. Considered a brilliant planner by all top managers, many of whom seek his counsel regularly. Would consider obtaining the CEO job to be the capstone of his career. Politically independent, but tends to take liberal positions. Eleven years in the company.

4. Joanne DeBernardo

Forty-four-year-old white female. Career as the corporate counsel. Also served as the head of the Federal Aviation Agency for three years while on leave from the company. B.A., Vassar; LL.B., Yale; LL.M. (in taxation), New York University. Married. One child at West Point. Second husband is a multimillionaire scion of an established, well-known West Coast family and is eight years her junior. Master at bridge. Health status is unknown. Appears to have a high energy level and jogs two miles daily. Has traveled to fifty-two countries. Speaks Japanese fluently. Dresses conservatively. Considered very innovative and likeable by employees at all levels. Conservative Democrat. Fifteen years in the company.

5. Edward J. Edgerton

Fifty-five-year-old white male. Career as the chief financial officer. Extensive experience in marketing. B.B.A., Northwestern; Ph.D. (in statistics), University of Chicago. Recently remarried widower. Five grown children and stepchildren. Completed psychoanalysis two years ago. Frequently testifies before Congress on the regulation of the airline industry. Ran for the United States House of Representatives six years ago as a Republican and lost a close race. Was born and brought up in the Philippines; family was interned there during World War II. Considered a serious but affable colleague and leader. In his spare time is writing a book entitled *The Economics and Politics of American Air Transportation*. Twenty-two years in the company.

6. John Arthur Fullmer

Forty-seven-year-old white male. Citizen of New Zealand. Career as an international general manager with a solid knowledge of operations in Hawaii, New Zealand, and Australia. B.A. with honors, Otago (New Zealand). Divorced. No plans to remarry and no children. Reports being in debt because of divorce. Likes traveling in the South Pacific and has toured every major island group. Pilots his own plane. Had a heart attack several years ago, but has recovered well and plays excellent tennis today. Considered by some to be a "crown prince" to the CEO job because of his business accomplishments in the Southern Hemisphere. Throughout his career has been highly regarded by superiors, peers, and subordinates, almost to the point that he is "bigger than life." Plans to become an American citizen. Nineteen years in the company.

7. Ernest "Skip" Gehrig

Forty-nine-year-old white male. Career as a general manager with in-depth knowledge of operations at all "hubs." Studied for three years in the famous P.P.E. (politics, philosophy, and economics) program at the London School of Economics. Six years later obtained a law degree by attending night school in Los Angeles, but never practiced law. Married to the daughter of the former president of Malaysia. Two grown children. Father was a co-founder of AIRSOPAC. Recovered alcoholic; has skin cancer but it is under control. Eight years ago was corporate vice president of personnel, but did not take the job seriously and performed poorly, considering the field "rinky dink." Was removed from the job by the board and then resigned from the board, perhaps in retaliation. Has twice absented himself from the company (on unpaid leave) to travel and study the economic potential of tourism in Samoa, Tahiti, Tonga, and other Pacific islands. Knows well many cultures of the islands because of his extensive travels. A maverick Democrat. Well liked. Dines occasionally at the White House with the President of the United States, who is a personal friend. Twenty-two years in the company.

AIRSOPAC DISCUSSION SHEET

1. Who was your final choice for CEO? for an alternate? What was your basic rationale for each of these choices?

2. What processes did you use to make your choices? For example, did you argue over personally preferred candidates? Did you vote? Did you use some type of rating system?

3. What specific elements of some candidates' career patterns led to the elimination of those candidates? What specific elements of the company's perceived needs led to the elimination of certain candidates?

4. Did any personal prejudices become obvious as you completed this activity?

5. To what extent did the candidates' personal and idiosyncratic characteristics influence your decisions?

6. Which candidate would be the least desirable CEO? On what basis did you make this choice?

CONTRIBUTORS

Gib Akin, Ph. D.
Associate Professor of Organization Behavior
McIntire School of Commerce
Monroe Hall
University of Virginia
Charlottesville, Virginia 22903
(804) 924-3847

Steven E. Aufrecht, Ph. D.
Municipality of Anchorage
Pouch 6-650
Department of Human Resources
Anchorage, Alaska 99502
(907) 264-4397

G. E. H. Beamish
Principal Training Adviser
Public Service Training Council
Chamber of Commerce House
22 Great Victoria Street
Belfast, Northern Ireland
30076

Guy Fielding
Senior Lecturer in Communication
Department of Communication Studies
Sheffield City Polytechnic
Totley Hall Lane
Totley, Sheffield S17 4AB
England
Sheffield (0742) 369941, ext. 220

Tim A. Flanagan
Assistant Dean of Students
Ashland College
Ashland, Ohio 44805
(419) 289-5003

Nancy Allen Good
International Student Affairs Consultant
20 Latimer Road
Santa Monica, California 90402
(213) 454-0575

Phil Leamon, Ph. D.
Professor, Multilingual/Multicultural Education
Curriculum and Instruction
College of Education
Florida State University
Tallahassee, Florida 32306
(904) 644-6553

Carol J. Levin
Consultant
2809 N. E. 65th Street
Seattle, Washington 98115
(206) 525-5072

James P. Lewis
Director
Effective Human Performance
6701 Johnsdale Road
Raleigh, North Carolina 27609
(919) 876-2817

Charles E. List
Management and Organization
    Development Consultant
Charles E. List Company
4940 Winterset Drive
Minnetonka, Minnesota 55343
(612) 935-3923

Michael Maggio
International Student Advisor
American Language Institute, JEF 251
University of Southern California
University Park, MC 1294
Los Angeles, California 90089-1294
(213) 743-2678

Thomas J. Mallinson, Ph. D.
Professor
Department of Communication
Simon Fraser University
Vancouver, British Columbia V5A 1S6
Canada
(604) 291-3687

Cyril R. Mill, Ph. D.
President
Behavioral Science Associates, Inc.
141 Wolftrappe Square
Vienna, Virginia 22180
(703) 938-0683

Janet Lee Mills, Ph. D.
Associate Professor of Human Relations
University of Oklahoma
601 Elm, Room 730
Norman, Oklahoma 73019
(405) 325-1756

Kenneth L. Murrell, D. B. A.
Associate Professor
Management Department
University of West Florida
Pensacola, Florida 32514
(904) 474-2308 or 2309

Thomas H. Patten, Jr., Ph. D.
Professor of Organizational Behavior
and Personnel Management
School of Labor and Industrial Relations
South Kedzie Hall
Michigan State University
East Lansing, Michigan 48824
(517) 355-4767

William J. Schiller, Ed. D.
President
Consolidated Counseling & Development
P. O. Box 4301
Pocatello, Idaho 83201
(208) 233-5596

Ron Sept
Communication Consultant
Department of Communication
Simon Fraser University
Vancouver, British Columbia V5A 1S6
Canada
(604) 291-3687

Bradford F. Spencer
President
Spencer & Associates, Inc.
2705 Maple Avenue
Manhattan Beach, California 90266
(213) 546-4523

Janet H. Stevenson
Associate Professor,
Communications & Human Relations
Secretarial & Administrative Studies Department
Faculty of Social Science
The University of Western Ontario
London, Ontario N6A 5B7
Canada
(519) 679-3731

Gilles L. Talbot
Professor of Psychology
Social Science Division
St-Lawrence Campus
Champlain Regional College
790, Neree Tremblay Street
Ste-Foy, Quebec F1V 4K2
Canada
(418) 656-6921

Alan Tolliday
Consultant
Department of Communication
Simon Fraser University
Vancouver, British Columbia V5A 1S6
Canada
(604) 291-3687

J. Allan Tyler
Program Specialist
Youth Services Division
70001 Ltd.
West Wing, Suite 300
600 Maryland Avenue, S. W.
Washington, D. C. 20024
(202) 484-0103

Susanne W. Whitcomb, Ed. D.
Associate Dean
School of Business Administration
California State University
1250 Bellflower Boulevard
Long Beach, California 90840
(213) 498-4504

Fred E. Woodall, Ed. D.
Associate Professor
Counselor Education and Psychology,
Box 3142
Delta State University
Cleveland, Mississippi 38733
(601) 843-3320

STRUCTURED EXPERIENCE CATEGORIES

PERSONAL
Vol.-Page

Self-Disclosure

Fantasies (16)	I-75
Graphics (20)	I-88
Personality Traits (349)	IX-58
Management Skills (353)	IX-93

Sensory

Awareness Expansion (19)	I-86
Lemons (71)	III-24
Relaxation & Perceptual Awareness (136)	'74-84
T'ai Chi Chuan (199)	VI-10

Feelings Awareness

Feelings & Defenses (56)	III-31
Think-Feel (65)	III-70
Frustrations & Tensions (75)	'72-5
Group Exploration (119)	IV-92
Expressing Anger (122)	IV-104
Projections (300)	VIII-30
Feelings (330)	'83-14

Feedback

Johari Window (13)	I-65
Analyzing & Increasing Open Behavior (99)	'73-38
Coins (23)	I-104
Peer Perceptions (58)	III-41
Puzzlement (97)	'73-30
The Portrait Game (107)	IV-24
Stretching (123)	IV-107
Payday (146)	'75-54
Adjectives (168)	V-114
Person Perception (170)	V-131
Choose an Object (198)	VI-7
Introspection (209)	VI-57
Affirmation of Trust (216)	VI-110
Cards (225)	'78-34
Developing Trust (303)	VIII-45

Vol.-Page

Giving and Receiving Feedback (315)	VIII-125
Feedback (355)	IX-107

Assumptions

Sherlock (213)	VI-92
Young/Old Woman (227)	'78-40
Pygmalion (229)	'78-51
Prejudice (247)	VII-15
Managerial Characteristics (273)	'80-31
Data Survey (292)	'81-57
Sexism in Advertisements (305)	VIII-58
Manager's Dilemma (331)	'83-19
All Iowans Are Naive (344)	IX-14

Values Clarification

Ideal Cards (143)	'75-43
Wants Bombardment (261)	VII-105
Banners (233)	'79-9
Louisa's Problem (283)	'81-13
Lifeline (298)	VIII-21
Introjection (321)	'82-29
Group Sell (357)	IX-114
Values and Decisions (361)	IX-146
The Promotion (362)	IX-152

Life/Career Planning

Life Planning (46)	II-101
What Do You See? (137)	'75-7
Career Renewal (332)	'83-27
Training Philosophies (363)	IX-159

COMMUNICATION

Communication Awareness Experiments (Oral)

One-Way, Two-Way (4)	I-13